practical DIVORCE SOLUTIONS

second California edition

by
**California Attorney
Charles Ed Sherman**

Nolo Press

P.O. Box 722, Occidental, CA 95465

This book is dedicated, with love, to my ex-wife
from whom I learned so very much
about the subjects in these pages.

Acknowledgements

Special mention—
Trudy Ahlstrom, who keeps the Nolo Press operation going in Occidental. She's good—I mean, folks, she's reeeally good, as were her invauable contributions to this book.
Lynda Barrad, who gave us so much warm support, good ideas and jovial encouragement.

Contributors—
I'm in awe at the number of people who have helped get the book (and me) this far, and grateful to have had the help of such outstanding people. Without them, it would have been a longer, harder job with much less to show at the end. It is impossible to rank them, so they appear in alphabetical order.

Thanks to:
• **Marje Burdine,** Director (and founder) of the Conflict Resolution Department at the Justice Institute, an arm of the Attorney General of British Columbia—for an exhaustive critique.
• **Rosemary Carter,** of Carter Communications, Vancouver, BC; a brilliant wordsmith and all-around good person to know (Bill too)—for keen editing.
• **Joel Edelman,** attorney, mediator, teacher—for insights into mediation.
• **Michael Fogel,** attorney, ex-judge from Los Angeles, metamorphosed into a new career in conflict resolution in Vancouver—for a valuable critique.
• **Betty Goldwater,** family counselor, Santa Barbara, a dear friend with deep insights and a great, generous heart.

• **Art Gottlieb,** attorney, playwrite—nepotism at its best.
• **Heather Hutchinson** and **Will Malloff,** dear friends in attendance at many a midnight debriefing.
• **Marty & Susan Hykin,** cherished friends, world-class minds—for fine feedback.
• **Jim Johnson,** Ph.D., Dean of Psychology turned entrepreneur and designer of applied psychology software—for incisive criticism.
• **Hugh McIsaac,** President of the American Association of Family and Conciliation Courts, an international society; Director of Los Angeles County Family Court Services; and a damn fine man —for information and insights into California's mandatory mediation and di-

vorce generally.
• **Tasha Schaal,** founder of Divorce Anonymous, a national support organization based in Los Angeles—for networking and moral support.
• **Lee Tuley,** Rennaisance Woman, brilliant keeper of the crystal heart—gives good feedback, and great ideas, too.
• **PGW,** Charlie and Julie and the whole gang for their consistent support and good ideas over the years.
• **Peggy Williams & Anne Lober,** Attorneys, mediators, and now partners in Divorce Help Line, for valuable critique and fresh ideas.
• **Teri Woods,** film-maker, songwriter, leprechuan, druid and, above all else, a bearer of the light.

CONTENTS

*"In a time of turbulence and change
. . . knowledge is power."*

—John F. Kennedy (1962)
paraphrasing Francis Bacon (1597).

1

How To Get
the Best Possible Divorce

The question now is not *if* you will get a divorce—the question is what *kind* of divorce will you have to go through? What price will you have to pay to get through it? How hard will it have to be on you—and the children, if you have any?

Isn't there some *good* way to get through it easier and cheaper?

YES!

We definitely *do* know ways you can make your divorce better. You know, of course, that no one can just wave a wand and make all your troubles go away. Divorce is never pleasant. But the right information can put you in control and make your divorce smoother, faster, cheaper, less aggravating and less painful than it otherwise might be.

This book represents information and experience accumulated from helping over 500,000 couples get better divorces through our *How To Do Your Own Divorce* books and services, together with the best ideas from dozens of professional studies. This information is tried and tested. It has helped others and it will help you.

This year, over 160,000 California couples will start the divorce journey. About 88,000 in Texas, maybe 70,000 in Florida—all together, nearly 1.5 million couples across the U.S. will start a divorce this year. So what? Who cares about all those other people? When there's a rock on your foot, you tend to lose interest in the view from the mountain. Yet, the fact is that you can benefit greatly from the experience of those millions who have gone before you. You can learn the best routes and how to avoid common traps and pitfalls. You can save yourself a lot of time, trouble, and money.

Start with the right information. Usually, people start into a divorce without bothering to find out anything about the rules, where they are going or how to get there. This is understandable, considering the upset of divorce, *but it is a very dangerous and costly mistake!* A survey of people who have used our divorce books shows that perhaps the single most important factor in having a better divorce is starting off with the right information, and having the control over your life that gives you.

So congratulate yourself. The fact that you are reading this book shows you have a desire to know and to participate that will lead you to successful solutions. That strength of character is one of your great assets—you are already on a good path.

The worst path and an alternative

The worst thing a person can possibly do is go off to some lawyer without any information or preparation and just ask for a divorce.

Want to know what happens when you go into a lawyer's office and you don't know anything? Well, first of all, how do you know you've got a good lawyer? And even the lawyer is good, how do you know you've got the right *kind* of good lawyer? It would be an advantage to know how to pick your lawyer, wouldn't it?

Then, how do you know what to ask for? If you don't know what you can get from the law, you might be expecting a kind of help that you can't get —or you might expect too much from the kind of help that you *can* get. Or you might not be expecting enough. If your expectations are off, you can end up frustrated and angry at your lawyer for the wrong reasons.

Next, the lawyer obviously has to find out about your case, so you sit there at $150 an hour telling practically your whole life's story because you want to get it off your chest and because you don't know what's really relevant to the legal issues—in fact, you have no idea what the legal issues are—and the lawyer has to sort it all out and untangle your story like a ball of snarled twine. Or, maybe be inhibited by uncertainty and clam up, leaving the lawyer to dig your story out of you bit by bit—at about $150 an hour.

Then you need to ask a lot of questions so you can find out what's going to happen and you probably have to go home to dig up some more information and maybe get some documents, then you have to take it all back for another office visit and ask more questions. This all takes a lot of time—at about $150 an hour.

And how do you feel? Ignorant and helpless.

Divorce tends to be undermining anyway, so it would be absolutely normal for you to feel insecure, inadequate, not in control of your own life. That's *before* you go uninformed and unprepared into some lawyer's office and reinforce those unpleasant feelings. It gets worse when you find out, as so often happens, that your lawyer is hard to reach and doesn't bother to help you understand what's going on in your case.

Now look what would happen if you knew what you were doing ahead of time—that is, if you had good information and were well prepared.

First of all, you might not have to go to a lawyer at all. If you *did* want a lawyer, you might be able to see one just for specific advice or for a limited service. In *any* case, you would know how to choose and how to use the right lawyer.

When you went in you would have your information and documents prepared ahead of time so you would just hand it all over and not waste much time on the facts. You would tell the lawyer exactly what you wanted to know and what you wanted to accomplish, and you would *not* have to ask so many dumb questions and feel helpless.

So you have already saved hundreds, maybe thousands of dollars, haven't you?

And what effect do you think this has on your lawyer? Well, the lawyer is very aware of dealing with a client who know's what's what—and you'd better believe *that* makes a big difference. You're going to get a whole different kind of treatment—better care and more respect!

And how does this feel to you, personally? Absolutely great! You are *not* helpless, you are *not* the victim of external forces. You *do* know what's going on, you *are* in control of your own life and you are doing a good job under difficult circumstances.

And what do you get? More respect! This time, your own.

Uncontrolled battle. The worse result of going uninformed and unprepared to a lawyer is that you are likely to end up in some sort of uncontrolled battle where the lawyer is in charge of your divorce—your life—and you are not. Contrary to what you might expect, it feels awful.

Even simple, unopposed cases cost a lot, but what's worse is that your case is likely to get stirred up into increased conflict and even higher cost. Fees of $2,000 to $5,000 for *each* spouse are considered very cheap for *simple* cases in Los Angeles, while $7,000 to $10,000 each is ordinary, and it can easily run well over $20,000 *each* if the case has conflict. In big money cases, a $200,000 fee on each side is no surprise. Of course, few lawyers start off quoting such figures; you are more likely to hear their hourly rate and an optimistic estimate. Fees aside, uncontrolled battles tend to drag on and on for a very long time, wearing you down, burdening your life.

Sometimes it is red-hot anger that drives people to call a lawyer, like pushing the ultimate button. You did show your spouse a thing or two, but you have also trapped yourself on the blind path to an uncontrolled divorce. Sometimes you are driven into it by your spouse's conduct. Either way, you end up there in a blind rush, uninformed and unprepared. This is what we want you to avoid.

The more emotionally distressed you are about your divorce, the more attractive it might seem just to turn the whole ugly mess over to a lawyer—but doing so almost never works out to your advantage. In the first place, lawyers don't handle the whole divorce, just the strictly legal aspects. Very few of your real–life problems will be addressed, but no one points this out, so you may have unreasonable expectations of what your lawyer can do for you. Then you suffer the frustration of finding out, eventually, that your problems have not been handed over after all—they've followed you home. They are still all yours, and you may have sprouted a whole new set of legal and financial problems as well.

Uncontrolled battle arouses the worst instincts in all parties. It will be very hard on you. If there are children, an uncontrolled battle is terrible, because children are always victims of the emotional and legal warfare between their parents.

If you don't know what's going on and if you can't control the legal game to your own advantage, you will face the financial trauma of uncontrolled legal expense. You will end up completely in the dark, an ignorant bystander in your own life. You will feel helpless ....and you may be right.

The alternative to the worst path: The only way to protect yourself and get the kind of results you want is to be fully informed and prepared *before* you begin, to be in charge of your own case as much as possible—which is what this book is all about.

How to get the best possible divorce

Three keys to a better divorce

Be informed and be prepared. The only way you can avoid the blind path that leads to an uncontrolled divorce is by becoming informed and prepared. It isn't hard and the results are worth it. People who know what's going on invariably get better divorces than those who do not.

Control your case. A Connecticut study (1976) showed that of couples with lawyers, about 60% worked out *all* their own terms without resort to their attorneys, meaning that in most cases the clients do most of the real work anyway. More important is a study in New Jersey (1984) showing that *client control of divorce negotiations is the most significant predictor of a good post-divorce outcome.* "Good outcome" includes things like better compliance with agreements, less chance of litigation, increased good-will, better co-parenting. This means that whether or not you use a lawyer, if you control your own case you will save money, reduce aggravation, and feel good about being in charge of your own life.

Taking control does not mean you can't get help or seek advice, it means that you take responsibility for knowing what's going on and for making your own decisions. You become an active participant in the negotiations. You take responsibility for your own actions and feelings. That's healthy and that's what works.

Keep business and personal matters separate. Many aspects of getting through a divorce are business-like in nature: money, property, procedures, negotiation and agreements, lawyers and taxes. Business and personal/ emotional matters do *not* mix well. The best way to protect yourself, to reduce conflict and confusion, is to keep business matters as separate as possible from emotional and personal concerns. This does not mean that you don't deal with personal and emotional matters—just not at the same time you are taking care of business.

2

The Divorce Roadmap
and an overview

Crossing the great divide

You can think of your divorce as having to go on a difficult journey across unknown, rugged territory—something like the early settlers faced when they had to get across the real Great Divide, the terrifying Rocky Mountains.

Behind you is a life you can no longer live. Before you is a future with more hope and possibilities, but first you have to get across some forboding terrain with traps, dangers and pitfalls. You stand there with your life's accumulations, fighting fear, trying to find the means and the courage to go into the unknown ....when suddenly someone shows up with a map and a book of information about the journey.

It may not be an easy trip, but you certainly do not have to go cross-country with no map or compass. Others have already marked all the best ways for you, and if you take a popular route there will be way-stations, traveler's aid services and even fellow travelers. What you need to do now is study the maps and the latest travel information before you start. You don't want to just wander off into your divorce, you want to go prepared.

So, like any good traveller encountering unknown terrain, you climb a tree to get an overview of the territory you have to cross. Okay, then—here's your map and a view from a tree.

Map notes

Study the map for a bit and try to get a sense of the possible paths you can take. The notes below are a brief summary of what each part of the map is about.

THE REAL DIVORCE: The legal divorce is a ceremony you have to go through, but standing as a constant background to the legal divorce is the "real" divorce. The real divorce refers to the emotional and

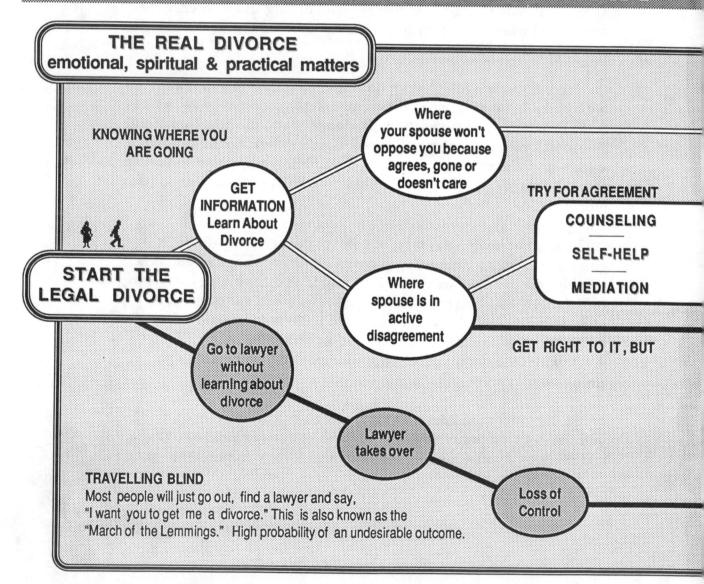

THE DIVORCE ROADMAP

THE REAL DIVORCE
emotional, spiritual & practical matters

KNOWING WHERE YOU ARE GOING

GET INFORMATION
Learn About Divorce

Where your spouse won't oppose you because agrees, gone or doesn't care

TRY FOR AGREEMENT

COUNSELING
——
SELF-HELP
——
MEDIATION

START THE LEGAL DIVORCE

Where spouse is in active disagreement

GET RIGHT TO IT, BUT

Go to lawyer without learning about divorce

Lawyer takes over

Loss of Control

TRAVELLING BLIND
Most people will just go out, find a lawyer and say, "I want you to get me a divorce." This is also known as the "March of the Lemmings." High probability of an undesirable outcome.

16

practical aspects of your life—areas barely touched by the legal divorce. This is about how you feel and what you have to do to get on with your life; about breaking old patterns and finding a new center for your life; doing your best with the hand you've been dealt.

Your ability to solve your practical problems will be greatly improved if you understand some basic things about the emotional stages you and your spouse might go through. Also, there are many traps in the emotional jungle that you can avoid if you are aware of

WHY TRAVEL WITHOUT A MAP ?

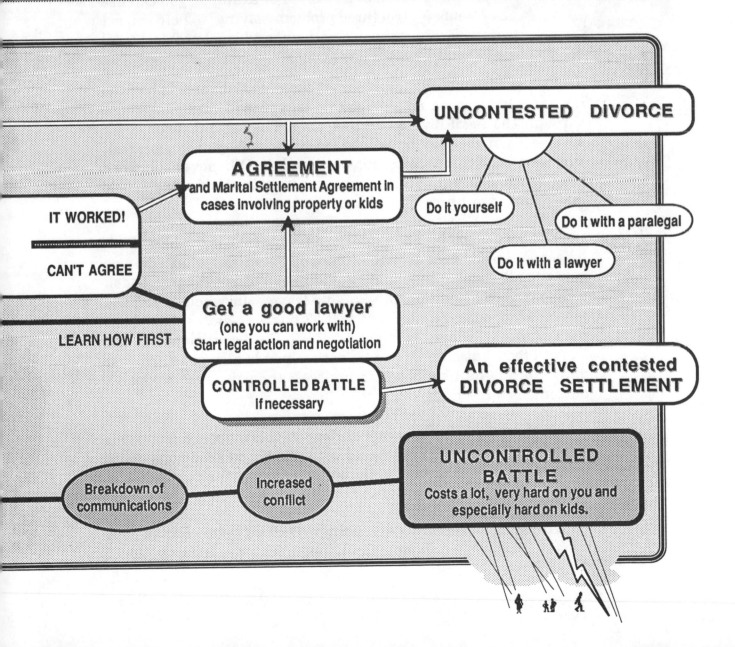

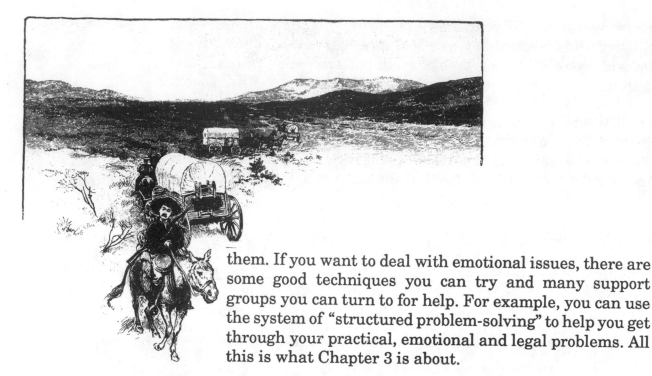

them. If you want to deal with emotional issues, there are some good techniques you can try and many support groups you can turn to for help. For example, you can use the system of "structured problem-solving" to help you get through your practical, emotional and legal problems. All this is what Chapter 3 is about.

THE LEGAL DIVORCE: No matter what your legal divorce is like, no matter what you do or how you do it, you will find your route through the legal divorce on this map. The legal divorce is far simpler than you may have been led to believe—you can see that there are only three main routes through it. Whenever there *are* complications in a divorce, they are always on the level of legal rules and red-tape or human relations.

The worst path: The route most people take is the blind path where you go into your divorce without any good idea what a divorce is really all about. You just go uninformed and unprepared to ask some lawyer to get you a divorce and leave your whole life in the lawyer's lap, hoping it turns out well. *This is the worst thing you can possibly do!* Of course, it might work out—and you might win the lottery, too—but success on this path depends almost entirely on dumb luck. The likelihood for unnecessary pain and expensive outcome is quite high.

One important option is not obvious on this map: if you start off on the blind path, it is often possible to get off and get on one of the better routes—but the sooner the better: as you go further along the blind path, it can get harder to get off.

Knowing where you are going: The two better routes both start when you learn about divorce, then work on your best options.

Notice that there are two branches of the better route—for cases that start with the spouses in active disagreement and cases where there is no likelihood of legal opposition from the outset.

Unopposed cases: Cases that are unopposed—where there is no legal opposition, that is—are relatively easy; they tend to go smoothly and can be very inexpensive. If you have this kind of case, you can easily do your own divorce or you can do it with the inexpensive assistance of a paralegal or a divorce typing service (Chapter 8).

Cases with disagreement: First, you have to choose—do you want to start by trying to work out an agreement, or do you want to go to a lawyer first and negotiate later. Are you playing hardball or softball? Before you decide, make sure you understand the overwhelming advantages, both financial and emotional, of an agreed divorce over a contested battle. Don't go to an attorney without getting informed and prepared first.

If your spouse is being bad or playing hardball, go straight to the best tough attorney you can find (Chapter 11) to take protective action. Try to avoid being rushed into an uncontrolled battle. If you *are* forced to take immediate action, read this book, get informed and take more control as soon as you can.

Most people will choose to work very hard to reach an agreement because it is worth it. You can help yourself a lot by learning conflict reducing techniques and, if you want to, you can get a lot of good help from counseling and mediation. But some people will decide they don't even want to try—they'd rather not deal with their spouse or their life that way. Either way, if you don't try for agreement or if you try and nothing works, the worst thing that can happen is that you end up in a controlled battle, and that is a whole lot better than an uncontrolled battle.

Controlled battle: This is what happens if you decide not to work toward an agreement or if you have tried and can't reach one. A controlled battle is a legal contest conducted with lawyers, but you know exactly what is going on. The issues of disagreement are well defined, and *you* are the one calling the shots. The worst outcome on this side of the map is far better and cheaper than what you are likely to get from going into things uninformed and unprepared.

Finding your way

Now that you've had your bird's-eye view of the terrain, take a look at these general directions for finding your way to a better divorce.

One: Study the territory. Learn how to deal with the real divorce in Chapter 3. How to take care of business (and yourself) is discussed in Chapter 4, then Chapters 5 & 6 tell you about the legal system and what you can get from the law.

Two: Get organized and get prepared. Learn how to do structured problem solving (Chapter 3). Clarify your interests, decide what you want. Use the worksheets in Chapter 7 to start preparing your case and yourself.

Three: Think about turning your case into one that is either settled by agreement or at least without legal opposition—then you can easily get an inexpensive divorce either by doing it yourself or with the help of a paralegal.
- Chapter 8 is about handling cases where there is no legal opposition. No matter how much conflict you have, you should read about unopposed cases to help you understand the advantages of agreement.
- Chapter 9 is about cases with disagreement or conflict. Learn about the various ways you can reduce conflict and avoid a battle. Try to agree, or at least agree to disagree peacefully.

Four: If you are playing hardball, or if you can't (or don't want to) avoid a battle, Chapter 10 is about how to wage and win a *controlled* battle—one where *you* are in charge and where you learn to fight effectively and to minimize the cost and damage.

Five: Learn how to pick the professional advisers you will use. Choosing a counselor or mediator is discussed in Chapter 9. Chapter 11 explains how to choose and how to use a lawyer to your best advantage.

3

The Real Divorce is Free

The state of your emotions has great *practical* significance. In order to make sound practical decisions—indeed, to solve any of your problems—you need to be very aware of your inner condition and, often, that of your spouse. You need to know how to deal with emotional issues and especially how not to get stuck in psychological traps. Understanding some basic things about how the real divorce works will help you enormously in dealing with yourself, your spouse and your list of practical problems.

This chapter and the next are about what we call the real divorce, with practical information and advice to help you get through it. The real divorce is about ending one life and beginning another, then making it work—spiritually, emotionally and practically. The real divorce is about making a new life and seeking a new center of balance.

Possibly the most real thing in your life right now is the way you feel. Nothing else in your life is as real as your pain, fear, anger, hurt, love, confusion, tension, nervousness, illness, depression—whatever it is you are feeling. The practical tasks you face are also very real—what to say to family and friends, what to do next, how to get by financially, and so on. The real divorce, then, presents these challenges:

Emotional: This is about breaking (or failing to break) the bonds, patterns, dependencies, and habits that attach you to your ex-spouse—learning to let go of fear, hurt, guilt, blame, and resentment. You learn about your old mistakes so you don't have to repeat them; you develop a balanced view of yourself, your ex-spouse, your marriage; you create self-confidence and an openness to new (and better) intimate relationships.

Physical: Our minds and bodies are *not* separate and life does *not* come in these neat boxes. Emotions—especially strong ones that are ignored, denied or repressed—are frequently expressed physically. During divorce, people tend to experience a lot of tension and nervousness, they get ill frequently and have accidents. This is a time when you must take extra good care of your health, pay close attention to your body, and be extra careful when driving.

Practical: This is about taking care of business on the physical plane—including the legal divorce. It's the nuts and bolts of what to do, where to go, how to get there as you begin to build a new life for yourself. You need to create safety and security for yourself and your children; to make ends meet in a new life-style that produces what you need and needs no more than you can produce.

In contrast to the real divorce, the legal divorce is specifically about peace, property, custody and support. It is a ritual ceremony that you are required to go through. What you end up with is a bit of paper with court orders written on it. So, what does the legal divorce accomplish for you and what does it have to do with the real divorce? Surprisingly little, as you will see; it is just a sub-category of the practical real divorce. But the legal divorce *does* have important symbolic value. When you file those papers, it makes an important statement to your spouse, to yourself and to the world that a decision has been made, that a new identity and a new direction has been chosen. In practical terms, it forces you to deal with at least a few of your important practical issues (property, custody and support). That's about it for the legal divorce.

The real divorce is what your life is about and how you go about it—it is your real work in life. And unless you decide to get counseling or go into therapy, the real divorce doesn't cost a dime. It is, however, very costly in terms of personal effort, but here, too, you can reduce the cost by learning to avoid the common traps. Going through major life changes—in other words, re-creating your life—is demanding, painful, hard work, but it may be the most important thing you can do.

Before discussing the problems and solutions of the real divorce, here's a very practical method you can use to organize and solve *all* of your problems.

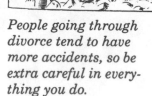

People going through divorce tend to have more accidents, so be extra careful in everything you do.

22

Of course, you should live your life whatever way seems right and best for you, but whenever you don't know what else to do, there's always this method to come back to.

Briefly, what you do is organize your divorce into a list of problems that you keep re-arranging in order of immediacy and importance. Then, from time to time you work on thinking up possible solutions and alternatives for each item, dealing with the most pressing problems first. Even emotional and life problems can be organized and solved this way, but the easiest to pinpoint will be the legal and practical ones. Just structure that part and you'll be way ahead. This method helps you to see exactly what you have to deal with and it makes the unknown take shape and become manageable.

First things first: The order in which you want to solve problems will, in general, follow the hierarchy developed by psychologist Abraham Maslow. He said that people have to satisfy their needs in this order:
- Physiological needs—hunger, thirst, fatigue.
- Safety—shelter, avoidance of pain and anxiety, general physical security.
- Need to belong and feel loved—affection, intimacy, family and friends.
- Esteem—need for self-respect, a sense of competence.
- Self-actualization—to be fully what you can be; to explore knowledge, curiosity, aesthetics.

When a lower need is unsatisfied, he said, all behavior tends to be directed to fulfilling it. If satisfaction is a recurring or continual problem, all the higher levels will fail to develop properly. You can use Maslow's hierarchy to help guide the priority of items on your list of problems.

For example, when hurt, any dumb animal knows enough to crawl into a den or a nest and just lay still and heal. People are smarter than animals (we are told) but they don't always know enough to hole-up, get very quiet and heal. Divorce can cause deep physical and emotional injury, so in the early stages of divorce, the first and most important thing you can do is to create *temporary* physical safety and security for you and any children in your custody. You need a place where, for a while, you can feel safe and a period of time to be relatively quiet, and relatively free of pressure and distraction.

What you are after *at first* are short-term solutions—think of weeks or a few months, not years. Don't try to solve all of your problems at once or create solutions that will last forever. Just take care of immediate needs, create a space for healing, and put the rest off until you have had some time to heal. Most of your problems will wait until you are ready to face them.

When you feel relatively clear and ready to start dealing with your life, begin to make a list of problems that you have to solve. Like this:
• Write down your thoughts as you read through this book, perhaps on index cards. Keep re-working your list as your understanding improves. Turn it into a diary or journal if you like.
• For each problem, make notes on additional information you need to get and resources you can use to help in the solution.
• As you work with your list, keep numbering and re-numbering the items in order of priority. Put your most urgent and most important problems at the top.
• Write down your ideas for possible solutions. Talk to your friends and family. Get ideas for solutions from this book, check out local family services and divorce support groups, or seek advice from professionals.
• Especially in the early stages, don't try for a final resolution of problems that can wait. Seek short-term and temporary solutions whenever possible. Don't do any long-term planning until your life settles down and you begin to see more clearly and calmly. Make a point of taking frequent vacations from problem-solving so you can relax.
• This is the most important part: be sure to balance your list of problems with a similar list of things you can use and things you have to be grateful for—your material and personal resources, assets, friends and family, health, and so on. Concentrate on your strengths: curiosity, love of life and people, desire to grow and improve.

If you do things this way, you will begin to see what you have to deal with. The whole confusing mess will have turned itself into a relatively short list of problems and each will have a variety of possible solutions. You may not be able to solve all of your problems immediately; few people can, but all you can ask of yourself is that you do your best with what you've got.

In scientific studies of life's most stressful events, divorce always comes in at the very top. Those-who-leave have different emotions from those-who-get-left, but the degree of turmoil is about the same. The important thing about upset is not *if* you are going to have it but *how* you are going to go through it.

How you go through your divorce is an expression of who you are. The way you deal with your problems will also determine who you will be when the divorce is long over and done with. "As the twig is bent, so grows the tree." You are creating your own future with every thought, word, and act.

Upset in divorce may range from mild to violent; it may feel like you've been physically torn—major surgery without anesthetic—or hit in the head, or just simply gone mad. Upset may last for weeks or it may linger for months, even years. *You can't rush things,* but you *can* avoid getting stuck in the common traps discussed below.

Your experience is unique—no two divorces are the same, but *everyone* goes through the same four stages in the recovery process. This is how human beings are built:

1. Shock: The first two stages might be so intense and disorienting that you feel literally insane, wondering if you can cope. Yet everything happens at once and you have no choice—you *must* cope, and you will. You might experience symptoms of shock, such as pain, numbness, feeling out of control or going crazy, loss of concentration, insomnia, extreme eating patterns. You may have wide swings in emotions. Intense anxiety, panic, anger, rage, depression may alternate with interludes of clarity, elation, optimism—and then back again. The shock stage can last from days to several months. It can be frightening and painful but it is *absolutely natural*.

The danger at this stage is getting stuck in denial and numbness, turning your effort to avoid pain and anxiety into a way of life. You *have* to feel, you *have* to grieve and hurt. Don't escape into drink or drugs; just let it happen. Trying to deny or avoid or run from the experience will only make it last longer. The depth of your pain is also the measure of your capacity for love and joy.

2. Rollercoaster: After the shock stage, the intensity tends to subside, perhaps become intermittent—this is the main difference from the shock stage—but you get confusing swings in emotions, especially your feelings for your mate and for yourself. You feel like you can't trust your feelings. Almost any little thing can set you off—a smell, a song, a memory. You dwell on the past, constantly reliving it and evaluating. You may feel guilt, blame, self-blame, anger, shame, loss, loneliness, or depression. The way you think about yourself is shaky and uncertain; you feel incompetent, awkward, inadequate, unlovable. Your feelings go around and around and around; they seem to never settle down.

This is all very natural, part of the grieving process, part of letting go of the past, and very necessary. It can go on for a few months to a year. You are under high stress and may be prone to illness and accident, so you have to take extra good care of yourself. Divorce is very much like recovering from major surgery. A big piece of your life has been removed. Be patient, be kind; pamper yourself a little.

Your judgment is likely to be poor while you are in this state, so try to avoid making important decisions. Unfortunately, this is exactly when you have to deal with your divorce and create new arrangements for your children. Put off making permanent decisions if possible; try instead for temporary solutions. Whenever decisions are necessary, try to make them during your calm interludes. Try not to be rash or impulsive. When in doubt, consult with trusted family and friends or stick to established standards such as those set by law. The middle of the road is safest on dark streets.

The mistake you want to avoid here is getting stuck. Your feelings are valid, but don't make a career of them. If you find that you are going around and around on the same themes, you will eventually have to stop spinning your wheels and wasting time.

If you dwell on loss, blame, or being wronged, you will prolong your own depression, anger, or fear. Don't get stuck too long—you need to get on with your life. Get out of your past and into your future.

3. Self-development: *Divorce is over when the end becomes a beginning.* The rollercoaster eventually evens out more and more. Now you begin to notice the possibilities of your new life. The present and the future become more important than the past. You pay a lot of attention to yourself and your image. You make plans. You make new friends, experiment with new interests and experiences. You may act like a kid again. Dating and sex may bring on a certain degree of confusion, a re-run of old feelings from as far back as adolescence. Have fun discovering what you are, who you are and who you like—but don't overdo it.

4. Emergence: You are getting comfortable with yourself, getting stronger, increasingly clear and aware of who you are. You are more interested in the present and the future. You have a new center of balance as a single person, whole and complete to yourself, and you are now ready for intimacy in new relationships. You survived the divorce and have been strengthened by it. You can still feel grief and sadness about the past, but without guilt, blame or resentment. You are no longer threatened by your own feelings.

If you don't get stuck, you will emerge. —definitely!

Remember that your spouse is going through these cycles, too. Whatever anger and grief your spouse is experiencing is helping to break the bonds of attachment. It is a necessary part of the healing process.

Let's take a look now at some of the major emotional components of the divorce cycle.

Pain: You have to recognize that pain is not only natural, it can be a helper and a good adviser. Especially at first, pain may only mean that you have been injured and are healing, as if you had broken your leg or suffered a grievous wound. But at other times it can be a message that something is wrong, that you have to pay attention to something you have been ignoring. The intensity of pain during divorce can be frightening, but you mustn't run from it or try to block it out or avoid it. To do so will delay your healing or even leave you permanently impaired in spirit. Instead, embrace it; let it happen. The pain is in your heartspace and that is where the real "you" lives, so it is calling you home to your center and to your real self. Endure your suffering, accept your pain and listen to it. If you do, it will run its course and heal more quickly; it will lead you to your solutions; it will provide the energy for your changes and growth; it will make you stronger.

Fear: The major challenge in any divorce is to deal constructively with your fear. Fear of pain, fear of hurt, fear of the future, fear of your ability to take care of yourself and your children, fear of losing self-respect, fear of fear. There is a basic bewilderment of life when so much is happening that you feel you can't possibly cope; you just don't know what to do or how to live. Fear is the root source of anger. Anger is the flip-side of fear. Anger turned inward is depression.

Anger: Learning how to use anger constructively is one of the most important lessons to be gained from your divorce. Anger is a potent source of energy and a very useful emotion *if* you know how to use it. Anger helps get you through the first and most painful stages of divorce by providing an outlet for inexpressible emotions and it helps break the bonds of affection and attachment.

For people who have never shown it, learning how to get angry is a huge step forward. Anger will help you to stop being dependent, stop being a victim. Anger and action are far better than making a career of being depressed, downtrodden, and helpless. You *can* learn to be angry, assertive and constructive all at the same time.

On the other hand, some people become addicted to anger and they misuse it badly. Anger soon becomes self-defeating and self-destructive; the cause of bad mistakes in judgment (like running to a lawyer before you are prepared) that will work against your own interests. Anger can drag you into an uncontrolled battle.

The attraction of anger is that it is cheap and easy—easier than actually solving your real problems; easier than taking responsibility for your own life. It is reliable, always there; you can count on it. For just a moment, it gives you a false sense of power and control; it lets off your steam. But anger is a solution that solves nothing. It serves only to distract you from having to face your own pain, fear or guilt. If you abuse anger, if you become a habitual user, it will poison your life and turn you into an unhealthy, lonely, bitter, spiteful person. You can count on it.

If anger is a personal issue for you and you want to learn to use it well, you will find some good reading on the subject listed in the Appendix. If anger and conflict are a major problem in your divorce, turn to Chapter 9 and read about how to deal with extreme conflict and techniques for reducing the level of conflict.

Hurt: It is a painful and terrible thing to be hurt by someone you depend on, someone you love and trust. In the early stages of divorce, you may need to heal from hurt that you have experienced, but you do *not* need to continue allowing yourself to be hurt. Someone can hurt you only if you give them the power to do so. Hurt then becomes something that you do to yourself, something you permit to happen. Staying hurt long after the divorce is over keeps you stuck on your needs and weaknesses; it reinforces your picture of yourself as a victim.

Healing

Healing starts with a lot of very little changes in your daily habits. If you take charge of the little things, the big ones will soon fall in line. You must see it as a triumph when you learn to do for yourself the little things that you always depended on your spouse to do, or make decisions in areas where you always used defer to your mate. Take pleasure in your new self–reliance when you learn to cook, take care of business, grow house plants, remember birthdays, mow the lawn, create an enjoyable living space, or keep the checkbook balanced. When you change your daily habits in the small ways, you are on your way up.

One of your great healing strengths is whatever it is that got you this far in this book—your curiosity, your desire to know things, a desire to take control of your life. Think about your other strengths and advantages.

Gratitude: Another major healing force—one of the most important—is gratitude. This is something you can work on intentionally. Focus on the things in your life that are right at least as much and as often as you dwell on problems. Several times each day, take the time to get quiet inside yourself and think about all the things that you have to be grateful for. Make a list; try to develop a strong sense of gratitude for your life and its many blesssings.

Self-reliance: Getting divorced means that you will no longer let your mate's moods and actions dominate your life. You are disentangling yourself from all the old patterns that didn't work for you. You can't control your spouse, but you *can* start to control your own actions. Learn not to react to your spouse's bad conduct and not to push back when your own buttons get pushed. Take responsibility for your own feelings, for your own life.

Acceptance and forgiveness: Possibly the most effective way to speed the healing process—the best way to achieve your own health and balance—is to completely accept your loss, feel your pain, and try to forgive your ex-mate and yourself. Guilt and blame are heavy burdens that can only hold you back and drag you down. Not forgiving keeps you stuck in a view of yourself as a victim. For your own sake, let it all go. Letting go is very different from repressing. You can't heal properly if you deny, avoid or repress your feelings—to the contrary, you want to feel your pain and loss. If you accept your feelings, they will run a natural, healing course; then you can forgive, let go of the past and get on with your life. Read more about forgiveness in books listed in the Appendix.

Support: Make an effort to seek out and use the help and comfort that is available from people in your life. You need the support of friends and family. If you can get it, use it. You can also get a lot of help from family services organizations, divorce support groups and single parent support groups. Make the effort to contact them; it may be very valuable and you have nothing to lose. For references, call the Conciliation Court service that is attached to the Superior Court in every county in California. You can also get references to support groups in your area through your church or temple, or from the California Self-help Center, a public service at UCLA, by calling 1-800-222-5465. If one group isn't what you want, try another. Then, there's the professional support that you can get from working with a good counselor. Chapter 9 discusses how to choose a counselor.

Get ahold of yourself!

In divorce, your emotional problems (looking backward) often disguise a great opportunity (looking forward). As Nietzsche said, taking a hard line, "That which does not kill us makes us strong." Another way to look at it is that you can learn a lot about what is really important in life and what your goals really are. At the very least, you need to learn not to create the same old patterns, not to repeat the same mistakes.

Pain is natural and unavoidable when you separate, but people have many ways of unwittingly increasing their pain and prolonging it. A lot of your pain may be entirely unnecessary.

Most unnecessary pain is caused by a very bad habit—negative thinking. There are self-defeating thought patterns that keep you stuck in anger, anxiety or depression. Whether aware of it or not, people are almost continually describing the world to themselves, and it's that quiet, constant voice that forms your attitude—your pre-disposition to experience things negatively. Don't be too quick to decide that you don't do this—it is so habitual that you may not even be conscious of it. That's what makes it hard to cope with.

Negative thinking causes you to paint your life in black with too broad a brush. The way you see things will be one-sided, overly-simple and unbalanced. Negative thinking keeps you boxed in, limits your possibilities, keeps you from seeing solutions and prevents you from moving forward with your life. What you think turns into what you feel. If you expect the worst, that may be what you get. Here are some classical examples of negative thinking:

- **Over-generalizing** is when you think or say things like, "You *always* put me down," or "I'll *never* find another mate," or "She *only* wants one thing from me." You have picked on one negative feature and made it into your total understanding. Try to stop using words like all, always, every, never, only, and totally, and so on.

- **Labeling** would be, "He's a selfish person," or "She's a bitch," or "I'm a loser." You pick on one negative quality and let that represent the whole person. This keeps you angry at others and disgusted with yourself.

- **Blame**-of-self and blame-of-others makes it seem as if the fault for your misfortune is all one-sided, but life is never like that and blame has unfortunate side-effects. If you blame yourself, you are trapped in guilt. If you blame your spouse, you make yourself a victim, avoid your own responsibility, and prolong your anger. That's all over now; the fact is that you each made your own choices and are responsible for your own actions. Now, get on with your life.

• **Filtering** happens when you see only the negative or threatening side of things. Focusing on your fears and losses will keep you in a state of anxiety or depression.

• **Catastrophizing** is when you exaggerate potential threats and stay focused on *anticipated* harm or disaster. "I'll never be able to pay my bills." "I can't survive this pain and loneliness." You expect the worst and don't expect to cope.

To avoid the consequences of negative thinking, you have to become more aware of your inner voices and attitudes. Try to notice when you are scaring yourself or seeing things through an all-black filter. When you catch yourself at it, stop. When the negative thoughts start again (and they will), catch them again. Keep at it. Don't be self-critical and put yourself down; just observe and be patient. Give yourself a little reward each time you catch yourself— a cookie or a balloon. Don't laugh, it works. Make yourself think in a more constructive vein: concentrate on solutions instead of problems, think about past pleasures, fantasize about future ones. Try to make yourself take a more balanced and rounded view of things. Stop and breathe, take a walk. Go get some flowers; make your space nice. Keep your attention focused only on things you can see, touch or smell.

This is very hard work and it takes a long time. Don't put yourself down if you don't succeed over-night. You can get a lot of help from a good counselor with this kind of work.

Basic elements of a successful divorce

Experience and academic studies have helped us identify the basic elements of a successful emotional divorce. "Successful," as used here, means completing the process of emotional separation, reaching a new center of balance as a single person, maintaining the welfare of your children, and establishing healthy attitudes toward yourself, your ex-spouse, and your past marriage.

Absence of conflict is *not* part of the ideal divorce. A degree of anger and conflict is natural, useful, even constructive. It helps to break the bonds of attachment and old patterns of relationship; it makes you think and reflect; it makes you change. But *excessive* and *destructive* conflict requires special treatment. The discussion of conflict and how to deal with it is in Chapter 9.

Apart from peace of mind, growth and other human values, there are very practical advantages to struggling as hard as you can to make your divorce better. The closer you can get to the ideals discussed below, the more you will ease tensions and conflict; you will have a far greater chance for compliance with terms of any agreements; you will save thousands in legal costs; if you have children, you will greatly improve co-parenting and cooperation. In short, everything works better.

BASIC ELEMENTS OF A SUCCESSFUL DIVORCE

Mutuality: Lack of mutual sharing in the decision to divorce is the primary cause of conflict in the divorce and post-divorce periods. In an ideal divorce, the decision is arrived at together. This does not mean that one spouse may not be sadder or more distressed than the other, but that both come to accept divorce as the best thing under the circumstances. The spouses should be mutually active in negotiating terms and in co-parenting. The most stable settlements occur when both spouses take an active role in the negotiations, not simply leaving it to a lawyer. A good divorce is an actively mutual enterprise.

Attitude: Each spouse should end up with a balanced view of the other spouse and of the marriage experience. There should be a sense of emotional and spiritual closure. You should be free of any lingering feeling of blame, guilt or failure. You want to create increased self-understanding, the ability to form healthy new intimate relationships, and a sense of self-confidence.

Children: In an ideal divorce, injury to children is minimized, primarily through maintaining good co-parenting relations. Children can literally be destroyed by fighting between their parents, so it is *very* important that parents be able to work together for the well-being of their children. When not resolved, conflict can go on for years, even after the legal divorce is over. *Children must be free of the feeling that loving one parent is a betrayal of the other.* They must be free of the thought that they are the cause of the divorce.

Trying to create the ideal divorce is like any other ideal you try to achieve, like ideal health or achievement in some sport. Your goals are something you work toward, but you don't want to beat yourself up every time you fall short. Just try your best. The closer you can get, the better and smoother your divorce will go, and the better your future will be.

Rules of the road for getting through a tough time

The important thing is to make up your own mind and take charge of your own life. You can't control anyone else, certainly not your spouse, but you do have control over your own thoughts, actions, and responses. Start working there. Break old patterns that don't work; learn new ones that do.

You have to do the inner work yourself. You can get help from professional counselors or friends or books, but in the final analysis you have to look inside for answers to life's problems. Whether you discover your own answers or borrow the best advice you can find from wherever you can find it, the choice—and the task—is yours.

Here, on the next two pages, are some rules of the road for the divorce journey. These are adapted from material developed by Sharon Baker for use in her family counseling practice in Rancho Palos Verdes, California.

34

Rules of the Road #1 —
Getting Yourself Through a Tough Time

1. You can expect to go through a cycle of
   - shock and denial
   - anger/depression
   - understanding and acceptance.

Then it goes around and around—many times—between anger/depression and acceptance. After a time, acceptance becomes stronger and lasts longer.

2. Let your attention focus on your loss; it is a good way to understand your pain. There is a message in your pain that will lead to solutions. Pain can give you motivation and energy to bring about changes.

3. Seek quiet and rest. Take extra good care of yourself. Exercise, eat properly, keep life as simple as possible.

4. Acknowledge and express your feelings. Talk to someone who knows how to listen. Keep a journal.

5. Seek out support from friends, family, clergy, divorce or crisis support groups, counselors.

6. Stay aware. Do not try to alter or numb your feelings with substances, such as alcohol, drugs, or overeating.

7. Be realistic in what you expect from yourself. It is normal to have mood changes, to feel confused, to have mixed feelings about your spouse.

8. Have faith in your beliefs and in yourself. Remember to be grateful for what you *do* have. Having life, you are a miracle of creation. You are alive, you can feel, you can learn, you can grow.

9. Work. Enjoy the benefits of a daily schedule and of accomplishment, especially in the small changes you are gradually adding to your life to make it better.

10. Be good to yourself.

11. Take time to be with adults and to enjoy social activities when you are ready.

12. Remember that healing is already in process. Time and nature are on your side. You *will* recover!

Rules of the Road #2 —
Getting Your Children Through a Tough Time

1. Tell children the truth in simple terms with simple explanations. Tell them where their other parent has gone.

2. Reassure them that they will continue to be taken care of and that they will be safe and secure.

3. Your children will see that parents can stop loving each other. Reassure them that a parent's love for a child is a special kind that never stops.

4. Spend time with each child individually. Whether you have custody or visitation, the most important thing to the child is your individual relationship with that child. Build the best relationship you can in your circumstances. The future is built of many tiny moments.

5. Children may feel responsible for causing the divorce. Reassure them that they are not to blame. They may also feel that it is their responsibility to bring their parents back together. Let them know that your decision is final and will have to be accepted.

6. Often divorcing parents feel guilty and become over-indulgent. Give your child love, but also give limits.

7. Your child is still a child and can't become the man of the house or a little mother. Continue to be a parent to your child. Seek other adults to fill your own need for companionship.

8. Avoid situations that place a child in the impossible position of choosing between parents:
   - Don't use your child as a way to get back at your spouse. Children can be terribly wounded when caught in a cross-fire.
   - Don't say anything bad about the other parent in hearing of a child.
   - Don't say or do anything that might discourage the child from spending time with the other parent.
   - Don't encourage a child to take sides.

9. You and your former spouse will continue to be the parents of your children for life. Pledge to cooperate responsibly toward the growth and development of your children as an expression of your mutual love for them.

10. Be patient and understanding with your children. Be patient and understanding with your self.

4

Taking Care of Business

The business end of divorce is about what you own and what you are going to live on in the future—your assets, debts, investments, cash flow, budgeting and taxes.

Divorce is an important financial event—perhaps the most important one of your life. The way you resolve your financial settlement, the choices and decisions you make now, can influence your financial well-being for the rest of your days.

Divorce is a time when you have to learn to take care of yourself, and you really do have to take care of business. This is where it starts. Try to spend *at least* as much time focused on business as you do on your emotional issues. Try very hard to keep business and emotional issues entirely separate.

In order to take control of your own life and make sound financial decisions about your divorce, you have to know what you want. In order to negotiate you have to know what you want. In order to tell your attorney what to do, you have to know what you want. The only way to figure out what you want is to know the facts and understand them. Then you have to know what both you and your spouse are entitled to by law (Chapter 5). Then you can make sound decisions about what you want.

First, gather facts and documents. Use the worksheets discussed in Chapter 7 to help you organize and understand your information. After you have all the information available, if you still don't understand your affairs, get help from an accountant, a credit counselor, a financial counselor or an attorney. Go over your facts with them until it all makes sense.

Knowledge is power. With it, you have strength and control. Without it you are helpless, a victim. Often, one spouse has more information and therefore more negotiating power than the other.

If there is an imbalance in bargaining power and strength between you and your spouse, the situation can be greatly improved with knowledge and information.

Your goals for the immediate future are to:
• gather facts, organize and understand all the financial aspects of your joint lives;
• understand your rights and obligations (Chapter 5);
• decide what you want;
• plan how to live on your new income in a changed lifestyle.

To get through your divorce, you will need to know all the facts and have all relevant documents in order, both for your own understanding and for your attorney, if you use one. If you get properly prepared ahead of time, you will have more peace of mind and you can save yourself thousands of dollars.

Common traps

Ignorance is the most common trap in the business of divorce. Because your life is upside down, you may not want to deal with tedious financial details, but if you don't take the trouble to understand what's going on in your own financial life and what you are entitled to, you might as well hang a big "victim" sign around your neck. Ignorance increases your own sense of helplessness and leaves you vulnerable to the risk of being manipulated, of getting a bad deal. You can seek advice and assistance from professionals, but you should never rely on anyone but yourself to take care of your business for you. Use the worksheets in this book to organize and understand your own business.

Bad judgment is a real hazard when emotions are running high, but let's face it, divorces are like that. Insecurity makes you doubt your own thinking and ability. Fear and anger make you grasp for too much or surrender too much. Of course, you should get what you are entitled to, but to demand more for emotional reasons is inviting a ruinous conflict that will leave you with less in the end.

Giving up what you have a right to can leave you with a future full of regret if not hardship. So be careful and take precautions against your own emotionally affected judgment:

• Understand the emotional cycles that *both* you and your spouse are going through (Chapter 3). Keep in mind that at any given time, emotions can strongly affect your judgment and decision–making ability.
• Keep business and emotional issues separate (see below).
• Don't jump to sudden conclusions or make impulsive agreements or decisions. Above all, unless you face a desperate emergency that can't wait, don't rush off to a lawyer until you have some information and get yourself prepared.
• Don't sign anything you haven't thought about or don't understand.
• Keep a journal and make entries in it regularly about your thoughts and feelings. Keep track of your evolving priorities, possible solutions to problems, and your goals. Review your journal regularly, especially before making any final decisions.
• **Use the legal standards as a guide.** You are not required to follow the legal standards (Chapter 5), but they have been worked out over millions of cases, so if you are confused or in doubt about what you want to do, use them as your guide.
• Seek advice from reliable, informed, experienced people.

Excessive spending is very common before, during and after a separation. At first, spending seems like a denial of the growing distance and disaffection between the spouses. A couple will buy a new home or remodel their old one, buy a car, take a long vacation, have a baby—anything to bring them together in something. This is not usually consciously planned, it just works that way. During separation, spending is used as an anaesthetic for emotional pain. After separation, the couple genuinely needs a lot of money to set up two separate lifestyles, added to which is neurotic spending driven by emotional upset.

Being aware of this trap may be of some help, but it is often difficult to see and control your own eccentricities. Control impulsive and compulsive buying the same way you would control neurotic eating habits. The best thing is to take every possible step to keep yourself open, centered and strong. Deal directly with your emotional issues instead of reacting and running from them.

Money–hiding is not common but it is not rare, either. Sometimes, when it becomes clear that a divorce is coming, one spouse or the other will start salting money away in a private money stash. If done without cheating the community, this is a good idea, because it gives that spouse a sense of security, independence and control. However, if community assets (that are half yours) are being secretly diverted into a separate account, this is a clear case of cheating. In moderate amounts, it may not be worth fighting over, but it is something to watch out for, keep track of, and include in any future accounting. In extreme cases, you will want an attorney to take emergency measures to protect the community estate and your interest in it.

Sometimes, the money manager will spend joint savings or take out a loan for living expenses while putting regular income into a separate account. A family business can be manipulated or run into the ground so income appears low later. Or bonuses and commissions can be postponed until after separation. The list is almost endless.

If a divorce is coming, take a careful look at plans to refinance your house or other kind of loan. Watch where income goes and watch your savings account withdrawals. After separation, take a close look at financial transactions during the previous year.

Keep business and personal matters separate

Divorce has a lot of business–like aspects (money, property, negotiation and agreements) and it is widely understood that business and emotions don't mix well. One of the best things you can do for yourself is to decide to keep business and personal/emotional matters separate—or as separate as possible. This will make a big contribution toward reducing the level of conflict and confusion in your case and in your own mind. Be sure to tell your spouse what you have decided to do and explain that it will help you both. You can benefit from taking this step unilaterally, but try to get your spouse to agree; set a good precedent by starting off with an agreement. Here are some guidelines:

• Work hard to decide what you want ahead of time. Postpone decisions on things you are not clear about. Keep a business diary for your thoughts and decisions and review it from time to time, especially before you go to a meeting.

• Be very business–like. Dress for business instead of casually, adopt a professional attitude and tone of voice. Try to see yourself as two separate people—a business professional and an emotional, feeling human being. Be the other person some other time. Postpone meetings if you cannot be relatively calm and thoroughly prepared.

• Discuss business at appointed times and places. Always be prepared with a written agenda of what you want to talk about and check off each item as it gets done. Bring copies of any necessary documents. Take notes.

• If you meet in person, do *not* meet at the home of either spouse. It is too personal, it triggers emotions, and someone may feel at a disadvantage. You should be able to get up and leave if necessary. Meet instead at a coffee–shop, in a library or school meeting room, at a park or a friend's house if it feels good. Anywhere quiet, safe and neutral will do, but do not meet at a spouse's home.

• You should refuse to discuss business and personal matters in the same conversation. Be consistent and diligent about this. If something personal comes up when talking business, say "I'd like to discuss that later with you, please," and offer to set a specific time for it. If your spouse persists, hold firm, repeat your request once more, then explain that you will leave or hang up if it happens again. If necessary, do so. Don't get excited or emotional; be business-like, but stick to your decision.

• Refuse to talk business when you are discussing personal matters. Do not get into a business discussion spontaneously or impulsively. You need to get properly prepared and emotionally composed each time.

• If your spouse is being difficult in your emotional life, try not to let that infect your business relationship. Similarly, if your spouse is being bad in business negotiations, don't let that affect you emotionally. Don't get upset—it's only business.

Money management—
two households on one income

This must be the most common of all divorce problems and a powerful source of fear that fuels conflict. Spending needs go up dramatically while income stays stable. If anything, the ability to earn money is reduced during this prolonged crisis, yet two households now have to live on the same old income. It is the unknown that makes us afraid of the future, afraid of change. What will you live on? How will you make ends meet?

Once your physical safety is assured, your next most important need is financial safety. The difference between a desperate existence and a good life is knowing that you have enough coming in and an emergency reserve that will see you through several months. Living securely on a low standard of living is far better than a higher standard of living that is always at risk. Many people don't seem to know that.

Once again, knowledge is power, the ultimate best solution. You will solve your money problems by using a budget to help you understand your situation and to make plans for the future. When the facts are clear, you will know what you have to do to be secure and live in balance.

Here is a seven–point system you can use to solve money problems and plan your future:

• Make an inventory of assets that you own, bills that you owe.
• Study your past spending patterns.
• Make an inventory of income that you can count on.
• Plan your future spending.
• Create a control system.

- Seek creative alternatives and set goals.
- Review and change.

Make an inventory of property that you own and bills that you owe. Use the Assets Worksheet discussed in Chapter 7 to help you organize and analyze your list of assets and debts. Your net worth is the amount by which your assets exceed your liabilities. If you own valuable property after your divorce, you may decide to sell it and use the money for living or for investments. As to debts, any budget you make will have to include a plan to pay them off or discharge them in bankruptcy.

If you find that you are overwhelmed by your debts and repayment makes your budget impossible, you may have to consider plans to reorganize or discharge your debts. Many cities in California have organizations such as Commercial Credit counselors (see white pages), a non-profit organization that will help you to consolidate and repay your debts. You can also consider discharging debts by declaring bankruptcy. Take a look at the Nolo Press book, "Bankruptcy: Do it Yourself."

Study past spending patterns. Use the Budget Worksheet discussed in Chapter 7 to help you organize and analyze your spending. Gather up all the old records, bills, receipts, checks and checkbook registers you can find covering at least one year. Some expenses are annual or irregular, so a shorter period of time may not give you an accurate picture of annual expenses. If not antici-pated, annual expenses (several hundred for insur-ance, for example) can create a crisis. Offer to make copies of records in your spouse's possession and offer to make copies of records you possess for your spouse to use. If your spouse won't turn over records you need, a lawyer can force them out through a legal process called "discovery."

If your records are incomplete, you will just have to make estimates from memory. By all means, start saving checks and re-ceipts from now on and, using the budget worksheet as a guide, keep a very precise record of your ongoing expenses over a period of time.

Most people have never analyzed their spending patterns and have never made any organized effort to control their spending. If your income is going to become reduced or uncertain, you may have to start some new habits. Consider it growth, an adventure.

Make an inventory of income that you can count on. Use the Budget Worksheet discussed in Chapter 7. What income can you count on? Naturally, you will need to be very aware of your rights or your obligations regarding child and spousal support. How much can you get? How much will you be expected to pay? What is reasonable? You should also be aware of the possibility that a spouse in need can go immediately into court to ask for temporary support and other orders that will be in effect until a final settlement by agreement or by trial and judgment. Support is covered in more detail in Chapter 5.

You should figure a low estimate for irregular or uncertain income, because if your actual income is low, your planning will fail and you will end up in a financial squeeze. Unfortunately, child support and spousal support (alimony) are, speaking *statistically* about cases in general, an inadequate and unreliable source of income. Spouses who regularly receive the full amount on time are in the minority. Fortunately, the problem has been recognized as a widespread social disaster and laws are getting increasingly aggressive and very tough on people who slack off on their support obligations. But be cautious about how much you figure to rely upon.

Plan your future spending. Now that you know how your money has been spent in the past, you are in a good position to make an informed estimate of spending needs in the future. Again, use the worksheet. You have to make sure that the spending you plan is no greater than the income you can count on.

If you occasionally take in more than you spend, that money should go to emergency reserves and investments for future security. Everyone should try to accumulate enough savings to live on for several months in case of an emergency. That's the only way to be secure.

If your spending needs exceed the income you can count on, you have only two alternatives: reduce your spending needs or find new sources of reliable income. Living on a lower standard of living is much better than the emotional stress and insecurity of living beyond your means. When cutting expenses, the worst place to compromise is in the food category. Your health comes first, but you can live very nicely on fresh fruits and vegetables, grains, and the occasional fish or chicken. Actually, that's the best possible diet, and it doesn't cost as much as packaged foods, fast-foods, and meals out.

If forced to, you can spend your savings or sell off assets to raise money, but these are non-solutions because you aren't solving your basic problem of more going out than comes in. When you run out, then what do you do?

Create a control system. A budget only works if there is some way to keep track of your spending and keep yourself within its guidelines. You don't need to label every penny, but you do want to watch your spending by budget category. There are a variety of methods you can use:

- Sort your income into envelopes by budget category. You can always see what's left to spend in each envelope and when you run out, you're out. The disadvantage is that you may not want to keep loose cash lying around.
- Keeping a ledger book of *everything* you spend is very accurate and works well, but fails if you let down or forget to enter any expenses. This is tedious and requires discipline, but it is the best method in most cases.
- Keep track in your mind. This is simple and works for some people who have simple budgets, but requires discipline and it's easy to make mistakes or fool yourself.
- If you are wealthy, you can hire a financial secretary who receives your income, pays your bills, keeps track of your expenses and gives you a personal allowance.

Seek creative alternatives and set goals. Now that you have a handle on your income and spending, you may want to set some goals for the future. Be as specific as possible. Creating a reserve of emergency funds sufficient for several months should be high on your list. Beyond that, you may want to consider a plan for investing in your future. If your budget is too tight or your income is too low, you will want to try to find ways to create more reliable income. This means looking for new work, more education and training, new opportunities, a new career. Read books on careers and consider seeing a career counselor.

Review and change. After your system runs for a while, you should sit down and review it carefully to see how it is working. Has anything changed? If so, you may need to change your budget. If you can't stay within a category, try to figure out why. Adjust and fine--tune your categories, revise your goals.

Problems? If you find the budget process too complicated or difficult, you may need to see a financial or credit counselor for help and support. Most cities in California have an office of Consumer Credit Counselors who will either help you or perhaps refer you to someone who can. Otherwise, you might ask your local bank loan manager or an accountant if they know any professionals who specialize in helping people with budgets.

5

What The Legal Divorce Is About

When you hear the word "divorce," most people think of legal things—what we will now call the "legal divorce." This chapter discusses each area of the legal divorce very briefly—what it is about and the decisions you will need to make. The law is discussed here in very general terms, just to let you know what to think about, what to watch out for, and how to understand your case. A more detailed discussion of the legal rules is found in *How to Do Your Own Divorce,* which is reprinted twice a year to keep it current.

Apart from legally dissolving the bonds of matrimony, the legal divorce is only about peace, property, custody, and support. That's it and that's all. What you get from your legal divorce is a piece of paper—a judgment—with findings of fact and court orders on the above subjects. That's all. If either spouse fails to obey the court's orders, you may need more legal action to get the orders enforced.

You may believe that a divorce (the legal divorce) will solve some or all of your problems. It probably won't. It rarely does, and it is critically important that you understand this so you don't expect too much from the legal divorce and set yourself up for frustration and disappointment. Never forget that you have to pursue real solutions to your real problems.

The law is used to impose a decision *only* when there is a disagreement that has been brought into court. If you can reach an agreement with your spouse, or if for any reason there is no *legal* opposition, you can get almost any terms you like without much reference to the laws. On the other hand, it can be very helpful to use the legal standards as a guide for what is fair and what will happen if you can't agree. Where children are concerned, judges will not rubber-stamp just any arrangement, but will look carefully to make sure your children are adequately supported and protected.

The legal divorce is about important, practical issues that you would want to deal with in any event, but you should be very clear that there are many other aspects of divorce that are not part of the legal divorce. Once you understand exactly what the legal divorce is about, you can focus on organizing your facts and making your decisions. As you begin to sort out your new life and your current problems, it is important to know what help you can get from the law and which problems you will have to solve yourself in some other way.

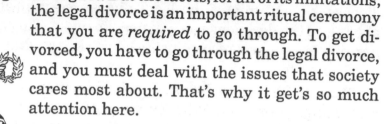

After all we have said to define the limitations of the legal divorce, it may seem contradictory that we devote most of the book to helping you get through it. But the fact is, for all of its limitations, the legal divorce is an important ritual ceremony that you are *required* to go through. To get divorced, you have to go through the legal divorce, and you must deal with the issues that society cares most about. That's why it get's so much attention here.

Dissolving the bonds

Even if only one spouse wants a legal divorce, there *will* be a divorce; you can't stop it. You can only have a contest on legal issues—the terms of the divorce concerning property, custody or support. One of the major traps in the legal divorce, the thing that leads to many unnecessary battles, is that people get so emotionally upset about breaking up that they fight over anything that can be fought over and have contests on the wrong issues for the wrong reasons. But the divorce goes through anyway.

California is a "no-fault divorce" state. This means that the court is not at all concerned with who is to blame for the marriage not working out—there's no future in trying to untangle that can of worms—but only with the facts and circumstances of the property, custody and support issues.

In California, a divorce is technically called "a dissolution," but we frequently follow the popular use and call it divorce. There are two other ways to terminate a dysfunctional marriage—separate maintenance and nullity. Separate maintenance gets you all the same orders for peace, property, custody and support as in a divorce, but the parties remain married. Some people have moral or religious reasons for not wanting a divorce, or sometimes there is an economic reason—such as where there are sizeable retirement, Social Security or Veteran's benefits to be lost in case of divorce, or where one spouse is a dependent under the other spouse's health insurance program and has a health problem that would cause a hardship if the coverage were lost. A nullity (formerly called annulment) declares that the marriage never existed at all, because the marriage was illegal or founded on fraud.

To get a divorce in California, one of the spouses must have lived in California for at least six months, and in the county where you file papers for at least three months just prior to filing the Petition. Being away temporarily, as on a business trip or vacation, does not count against your residency time.

There is an imposed waiting period, just in case you cool down and change your mind. Whenever you get your divorce orders, they will go into effect immediately, but the marriage itself is not technically dissolved until at least six months after the date the Petition was served on the Respondent spouse.

Keeping the peace

AUTOMATIC RESTRAINING ORDERS: In California, *every* dissolution contains automatic restraining orders. With service of the Summons, *both* spouses are ordered not to:
- harass, assault or disturb the other spouse;
- remove a child of the parties from the state without written permission of the other spouse or consent of the court;
- encumber or transfer any property except in the usual course of business or for necessities (like paying your divorce attorney);
- cancel or transfer any insurance held for the benefit of either the other spouse or a minor child.

These orders are in effect between the date the Summons is served and the date you get your Judgment, so if you need even one of these protections in your case, you should get the Summons served on your spouse as quickly as possible.

In special cases, you may want to go to court for additional or stronger orders, for example, getting your spouse ordered to move out. If there are children, special orders can be made for visitation away from the family premises and, if necessary, through a third person. Restraining orders will often help control a bad situation, but not always—sometimes you have to find a way to help yourself.

The legal remedy (discussed more in Chapter 9) is just one of many possible solutions, such as counseling and self-help. Self-help includes learning new response patterns, joining a support group, calling on friends, clergy or the authorities for help, moving away, hiding, taking karate classes, and so on. Your own attitude is actually the most important ingredient in any solution.

Property

California is a community property state. Our basic philosophy is that a husband and wife are equal partners in life so whatever either spouse earns or accumulates during the marriage belongs to them both equally. It doesn't matter if one spouse earns wages while the other stays home—they are doing life together as partners, so they share anything that comes in.

In California, there are two kinds of property: community property and separate property. "Property" includes not just things you own, but also your debts—a negative form of property.

• **Separate property** belongs to just one spouse and not the community. Generally speaking, separate property is a) property that was acquired *before* the marriage, and b) property that was given specifically to one spouse by gift or inheritance at *any* time. Separate property is not divided because it already belongs entirely to one spouse or the other.

• **Community property** is, generally speaking, anything earned or acquired by either spouse during the marriage that is not separate property. Community property belongs to both spouses equally, so each spouse is entitled to an equal share when there's a divorce. This includes debts incurred by either spouse up to the time of separation.

Joint title: Property acquired during marriage in any form of joint title (both names on it) is presumed to be community property *unless* there exists a written agreement otherwise.

Don't forget about accumulated vacation pay, pension funds, profit sharing schemes, stock plans, tax refunds and equity in insurance policies. You are entitled to half of whatever value was accumulated in these accounts during the marriage.

Problem Areas: The general rule is simple and clear. You just list the community property, value it and divide it so each spouse gets half. But there are exceptions and problem areas that you need to know about. If, for example, separate and community property were mixed, it can be difficult to unravel. This is a dark corner where arguments can be born. Another problem area is where spouses made agreements or understandings that were intended to change the nature of their property. Lets take them one at a time.

Commingling is what happens when separate property is mixed into the community so thoroughly that it cannot be traced, like mixing salt and pepper together—you can see they've been mixed, but there's no way you can sort it out again. If separate property was used for community expenses, and if it cannot be clearly traced, it is considered to have been a gift to the community.

Transmutation is the legal term for what happens when separate property is changed to community property or vice-versa. Before January 1, 1985, the change could be made by oral agreement or understanding. After that date, if the sentiment was not put in writing, it doesn't count—separate property does not lose its character as long as it can be clearly traced.

Tracing and reimbursement. There might be a right to reimbursement if separate property was used to buy or improve a community asset. Before January 1, 1985, there was no such right unless you can prove an agreement or understanding about it. But after that date unless there was a *written* agreement to the contrary, there *is* a right to reimbursement. The right to reimbursement depends upon the ability to trace very clearly where the funds came from and where they were spent.

Conversely, if community assets were used to buy or improve a separate property, the community has a proportional interest in that separate asset. Also, the community may be entitled to reimbursement for 1) contributions to the education or training of a spouse that substantially increases that spouse's earning ability, and 2) payments for support obligations from a previous marriage, but only to whatever extent the person who owed the support had separate assets available that were not used.

If your estate is tangled and complex, you might need to get some legal advice to help untangle it. If there is a disagreement between the spouses, don't hesitate to get several opinions. Try to settle disagreements on the gray areas according to personal values and understandings. Admit that there is room for a difference of opinion. Weigh the amount involved against the cost of a legal battle over it—will it cost more to fight than to compromise?

Get organized and make decisions: In order to get through a legal divorce, you have to itemize, characterize, value, and divide all your property. The Assets worksheet in Chapter 7 will help you do this. You will need to develop the following information:

- Itemize: what property do you own?
- Characterize: which items are community property and which are separate property?
- Value: how much is the community property worth?
- Divide: how will we divide the community property?

Itemize: Make a detailed list of everything of value you own. Small items can be grouped together under a general item heading, such as "jewelry," or "household goods," or "sports equipment."

Characterize: This means labeling each item as either separate or community property. To determine who owns what, you may need to know more about the laws and how they apply to the facts in your case. Start by reading *How To Do Your Own Divorce*, then, if you still have questions, you can get legal advice specifically on this question, or call Divorce Help Line (1-800-359-7004).

Value: You need to establish the "fair-market value" of your community property. This does not mean what you paid for an item or what it is worth to you or what it will be worth some day. Fair-market value means what you would get if you sold the property on the open market on the date it is being divided. There is a lot of room for differences of opinion on value, so this is something you would ideally want to work on with your spouse; at least communicate about it so your spouse doesn't think you are trying to be sly. Differences of opinion can be settled by using a professional appraiser. You will need an appraisal anyway for large or hard-to-value items, such as real property, pensions or a going business.

Divide: Community property is divided equally unless the spouses agree otherwise. Separate property does not get divided because it already belongs to just one person, but it is a *very* good idea to list and confirm the ownership of valuable or special items for the record and for the sake of clarity in the future.

Community and separate property can be divided any way you and your spouse see fit—if you do it by agreement. If you can't reach an agreement, your property will be divided by a judge according to law. In California, the laws are so detailed that, once all the facts are known, the way a court will divide your property can usually be predicted ahead of time with fair accuracy. This means that in most cases, you might as well agree to something within the predicted range, because a battle over property will almost always cost more than you can possibly gain by fighting over it.

THE FAMILY HOME and other real estate: Deciding what to do with a family home is both an emotional and a financial decision. If the home is otherwise a sound investment, owning it can represent security and stability. On the other hand, it may be full of memories and ghosts of the past, so it may be bad for you emotionally to stay in it. On the other hand, if you have children, it may be better if they stay in a house, neighborhood and school system they are used to. On the other hand, you could sell the house, move to a more modest accommodation, and invest the money you have saved. Will your decision lock you into your past or will it represent a sound financial investment? You get to decide.

The value of what you own in real estate is called your "equity"— the amount you can actually sell it for on the open market less all amounts owing on it and less the cost of sale. If community funds were used to buy, improve or make payments on any real estate, then the community has some interest in it and each spouse is entitled to half of the community interest. If you have a community interest in a house or other real estate, you will have to understand the rules and tax consequences so you can make your decision. First, read *How to Do Your Own Divorce* to learn the rules, then, if that isn't enough, consult an attorney, or call the Divorce Help Line.

INCOME AND DEBTS: Income and accumulations of either spouse after the date of separation are their own separate property, whether or not any legal action has been filed. An exception would be retirement benefits or any other form of delayed income that was earned, at least in part, during the marriage.

Debts from before marriage are the separate property (and responsibility) of whoever incurred them. Loans for the education and training of one spouse are treated as the separate property of that person. In general, you are not responsible for your spouse's debts after separation, *except* that you can be liable for your spouse's debts incurred for the "common necessaries of life"—food, clothing, shelter, medicine—*unless* you have a written waiver of support or have settled the matter in court. So hurry up and get on with the legal divorce!

You could be responsible for accounts that are in both of your names or to merchants who are used to extending credit to you as a couple. This is why it is very important for you to close or remove your name from all joint accounts and credit cards, and give written notice to creditors that you have dealt with as a couple. Tell them that you will no longer be responsible for debts of your (ex) spouse. Be sure to notify your spouse ahead of time when you close accounts or take other steps that could have an effect on his or her life.

You must understand that you will always be liable for any debt for which you were liable when it was originally incurred. That means that orders of the court and agreements between spouses about who must pay which debts are only effective between the spouses and do not affect the creditor's rights. If a debt incurred during marriage is assigned by court order to your spouse and your spouse fails to pay it, you are still obligated.

Date of Separation affects the character of both income and liability for debts, yet this is an ambiguous date, both emotionally and legally. The date of separation is when there has been a true breakdown in family relations with no present intention of carrying on the marital relationship. This is subjective; at least one spouse must intend to remain separate forever. Moving out and not sleeping together are very important pieces of evidence but do not of themselves determine the issue. Fortunately, in most cases it won't particularly matter whether it was one month or another, but occasionally the date will have important financial consequences.

Ten ways to divide property without a fight

The following list was developed by Superior Court Judge Robert K. Garst of Riverside County as an aid to spouses having trouble reaching agreement.

1. Barter: Each party takes certain items of property in exchange for other items. For instance, the car and furniture in exchange for the truck and tools.

2. Choose Items Alternately: The spouses take turns selecting items from a list of all the marital property, without regard for the value of items selected.

3. One spouse divides, the other chooses: One spouse divides all community property into two parts and the other spouse gets the choice of parts.

4. One spouse values, the other chooses: One spouse places a value on each item of community property and the other spouse gets the choice of items totaling one-half of the total value.

5. Appraisal and alternate selection: A third person (such as an appraiser) agreed upon by the parties places a value on contested items of community property and then the parties choose alternately until one spouse has chosen items worth half the value of the community property.

6. Sale: Some or all of the community items are sold and the proceeds divided.

7. Secret bids: The spouses place secret bids on each item of community property and the one who bids highest for an item gets it. Where one receives items that exceed 50% of the total value, there will be an equalization payment to the other spouse.

8. Private auction: The spouses openly bid against each other on each item of community property. If one spouse gets more than 50%, an equalization payment will be made.

9. Arbitration: The spouses select an arbitrator who will decide the matter of valuation and division after hearing from both spouses and considering all evidence.

10. Mediation: The spouses select a mediator who works to help them reach an agreement on the matters of valuation and division.

If you have children, you will have to create a parenting plan—a detailed understanding of your arrangements for the future care of your children. This is a difficult issue for divorcing parents yet it is the most important matter you deal with. It is critically important that you resolve the parenting relationship with a minimum of bad feeling and a maximum of cooperation. Children need both of their parents and the parents need all the help they can get from each other in the future. Harm to children from divorce is more closely related to conflict *after* the divorce so your goal is to make arrangements that both parents can live with agreeably. See Chapter 9, Protecting Your Children. It is important to try to avoid anything that makes either parent feel he or she is "losing" the child to the other parent. A child is not an object to be won or lost.

Before you do anything else, read *How to Do Your Own Divorce*, to learn the updated rules of law related to child custody, then start communicating with your children's other parent to see what will work best for the children and still be comfortable for both of you. To help with your negotiation and planning of child custody matters, use the Parental Activity worksheet in Chapter 7. It will give you a realistic view of how child-rearing chores have been shared in the past and how you intend to share them in the future.

Experience shows that pure joint custody—sharing parental rights and responsibility equally—only works well for parents who are cooperative and capable of working out future scheduling problems as they come up. For most parents, the most popular and successful parenting plan provides for joint legal custody for both parents, primary physical custody for one parent, and a highly detailed schedule that shows in great detail exactly when the other parent will have custody of the child. This provides stability while helping reduce the sense of alienation and loss of the out-parent. Finally, there is the tradional award of primary physical *and* legal custody to one parent with a visitation schedule for the other.

After judgment, parents can depart from their own parenting plan and work out their own arrangements informally, by agreement. The plan is most useful to create stability, security and to settle potential disagreements about who is to do what and when. This is why the plan should be as detailed as possible.

Mandatory mediation: If the parents cannot agree on a parenting plan, the matter will have to be decided in court. However, before a custody dispute can get to trial, the parents are *required* to meet with a court mediator who will try to help the parents reach an agreement. When and for how long these sessions take place varies from county to county. If you have already been to a private mediator, the court mediator will evaluate the effort and may decide that you have already satisfied the requirement. The content of your communication with the court mediator is completely confidential, but some counties do require the court mediator to make recommendations to the court.

If you have trouble working out an agreement on custody and visitation, you should seriously consider mediation. Court mediators have been very successful even though they can only spare a few hours per case. Los Angeles court mediators, for example, settle over 60% of their hard-core dispute cases. Private mediation should be considerably more successful because you are doing it voluntarily and you can spend more time at it.

After the divorce, if co-parenting does not work well, you should seriously consider professional counseling to help the two of you work better at co-operative co-parenting. You can also get a lot of help from the many parenting support groups and family service agencies throughout California. Call your county Superior Court and ask for the Conciliation Court service, then ask for a reference, or call the California Self-Help Center at 1–800–222-5465 for self-help referrals throughout California.

Support

Support for children and spouses usually raises the inescapable fact that the same old family income now has to support two separate households. Obviously, some significant changes in lifestyle are going to be made, and the spouse that was least in favor of the divorce will be most angry and begrudging about the "forced" changes. Less than half of all support orders are actually paid in full and on time. These facts of life reinforce the proposition that you should work very hard to get mutual consent to the divorce and agreement to the terms of the divorce.

If child or spousal support will be an issue in your case, start by reading *How to Do Your Own Divorce* to learn the updated legal rules on this subject, then get all your financial information together by filling out the forms in Chapter 7 and the Financial Forms in *How to Do Your Own Divorce*. Then you can negotiate.

Each county in California has guidelines for child and spousal support that judges refer to and follow in most cases. These guides are incorporated in computer programs that are widely used by judges and family law attorneys. If you refer to the guidelines ahead of time, you can fairly accurately predict the level of support that will be awarded in a court contest. So why fight or argue? Just check the guidelines. Unfortunately, the guidelines are generally not widely published—you have to dig them out of the county law library—and when you do get them, you will find that they are very complicated. The best thing you can do is to take all your financial information to a family law attorney and get an opinion on the level of support that would be awarded in your case. You can get the same information by calling us at Divorce Help Line (1-800-359-7004).

Child support orders are always subject to modification, which means that either parent can go back to court at any time to seek a change in the orders. To get a modification, it is necessary to show that needs or circumstances have changed since the last order.

If there are children, child support will have priority over spousal support. Only after the needs of children are satisfied will the courts consider an award of spousal support. Then the court willtry to balance the needs of one spouse against the ability to pay of the other.

The Budget worksheet in Chapter 7 is essential for working on your financial planning. Don't let this slide. Budgeting can be quite tedious and difficult but, especially now, it is *very* necessary. If you have trouble with it, you should seek the help of a financial counselor. To find one, look in the white pages for Consumer Credit Counselors, ask the Better Business Bureau, ask your local bank loan officer, or ask an accountant for references. Or you can call us at Divorce Help Line (1-800-359-7004).

Tax issues

There may be important tax consequences around any aspect of divorce that involves money or property—the division of community property, terms of spousal and child support, exemptions for children, child care tax credits, deductions for legal expenses, medical expenses, and tax returns filed during the separation period. Depending on how much money and property you have, you could possibly save a lot of money by seeing a good tax expert, especially before making a marital settlement agreement.

The Federal and California tax laws are somewhat different and both are so extremely complex that many divorce lawyers must frequently get expert advice, so a detailed treatment here is not only beyond our scope but also pointless because tax laws change constantly.

The first thing you should do is go to a local IRS office and get a *current* copy of publication number 504, "Tax Information for Divorced or Separated Individuals." This will tell you a great deal of what you need to know, but the print is small and the language is bureaucratic. If you have a lot of income and property, it will pay you to get expert advice about ways you can save on taxes. See a local attorney, or call us at Divorce Help Line (1-800-359-7004).

Learning more about the law

In some cases, you will want to know more about the laws and how they apply to the facts of your case. There are four easy sources of information on this subject.

• The cheapest and easiest thing you can do is read the book *How To Do Your Own Divorce*. A more detailed discussion of the law relevant to uncontested divorce is in that book instead of this one because the law can change as often as twice each year. *How To Do Your Own Divorce* is kept up to date and revised whenever there are changes. You can borrow a copy from your library, buy it at your book store or order it from us, but make *sure* you use a *current* copy.

• Go to a lawyer and pay for your information, but first be sure to read about choosing and using a lawyer in Chapter 11. Getting information from a lawyer can be relatively reasonable and efficient if you go prepared and have specific goals in mind. Learn as much as you can ahead of time.

Working through Chapter 7 before your first visit to a lawyer will get you prepared. The clearer and more informed you are, the faster and cheaper you can get what you need. If you don't know what you want to find out, or if you can't make up your mind about things, wait until your mind clears. Otherwise you may end up paying $150 an hour for hand-holding, or you may get talked into legal action you don't need.

• Call us at Divorce Help Line (1-800-359-7004) and talk to our staff of divorce specialists—attorneys, mediators, counselors, and paralegals—about anything at all to do with your divorce. We can help you with legal information, advice, and paperwork at rates that are lower than charged by most attorneys in California. As with using attorneys, the more prepared you are before you call, the lower your costs will be.

6

How The Law Works

Anatomy of a divorce case

Cases with no legal opposition are called "uncontested." These are relatively simple to process. Cases where the spouses are in legal opposition are "contested" and will stay contested until all issues are resolved either by agreement or trial. They are not at all simple to process. Take a look at the illustration, "Anatomy of a Divorce," on the next page. Just a glance is enough to see the relative simplicity of an uncontested case and the extreme complexity of a contested case that goes all the way to trial.

All divorces start with the filing of a Petition that gets served on your spouse to give notice of the suit. It contains your statement of the facts of your case and the outcome you are seeking. Other forms and legal documents must also be filed, depending on state and local requirements. From this point on, the difference between a contested and an uncontested case is dramatic.

In order to contest the Petition, a Response has to be filed within 30 days from the date the Petition was served on the Respondent spouse, and the case then becomes "contested." If there is no legal response to the Petition, it is assumed that the Respondent concedes all issues according to the broad terms of the Petition and the case is "uncontested." A contested case can become uncontested at any time an agreement is reached or if either side simply drops out of the contest.

The uncontested divorce goes straight to a routine hearing and judgment. Some couples will want to work out a written marital settlement agreement along the way, but this is optional. That's it, and that's all there is to it.

In California, the court hearing is *usually* not necessary, as most uncontested divorces can be processed by submitting a signed,

61

sworn declaration and the judgment will be returned by mail. This works because uncontested cases are invariably so boringly routine that it isn't necessary to take up valuable court time with them.

There's a surprising thing about legal procedures —no matter how complex they may appear, there is usually a relatively simple, routine way to handle the mainstream of "ordinary" cases. This is inevitable because bureaucrats, clerks, lawyers and judges—all ordinary human beings—need to process their heavy case loads with a minimum of thought and effort. Uncontested divorces are almost always routine. The more ordinary your case appears to be, the easier it will be to breeze through without a wrinkle. Almost anyone can do their own uncontested divorce (see Chapter 8).

Contested divorces are another matter entirely. Take a minute now to study the diagram of a contested divorce in the illustration. There are lots of steps and each step is quite complex— worth a chapter or a book of its own. A contested divorce can scarcely be understood, much less handled, by anyone without legal information and experience.

Advantages to a legal contest: It might seem odd after all we have said, but there *are* some advantages to starting a contested divorce:

• You can request immediate, temporary orders for getting possession of the family home, or for child custody and support. If you are stranded without income or money to live on, this is your best course of action.

• You can immediately freeze all accounts and get an order forbidding new loans, debts, or waste of community assets.

• You can use powerful legal tools to get documents and facts under oath.

• Many people find it easier to accept a judgment rather than go through the pain and effort of negotiating with their mate.

• Fighting is an outlet for or a diversion from the pain of divorce and it can help to sever bonds of attachment and affection—it distances you from your spouse very effectively.

• There is the chance for vindication and material gain—*if* you win.

• And finally, some people just feel like fighting.

ANATOMY OF A DIVORCE

CONTESTED CASES

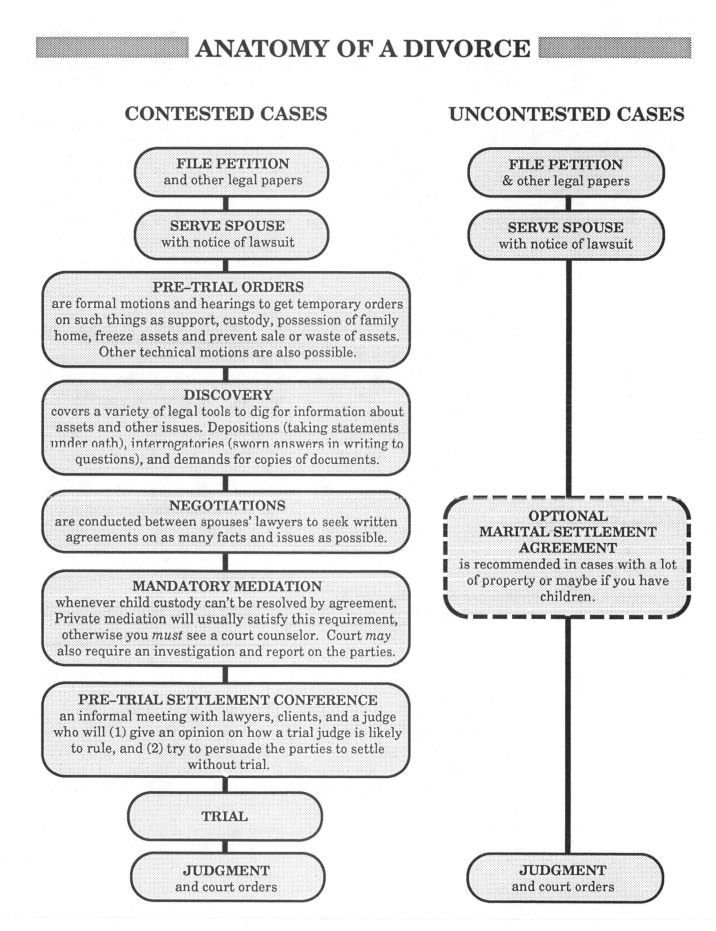

FILE PETITION
and other legal papers

SERVE SPOUSE
with notice of lawsuit

PRE–TRIAL ORDERS
are formal motions and hearings to get temporary orders on such things as support, custody, possession of family home, freeze assets and prevent sale or waste of assets. Other technical motions are also possible.

DISCOVERY
covers a variety of legal tools to dig for information about assets and other issues. Depositions (taking statements under oath), interrogatories (sworn answers in writing to questions), and demands for copies of documents.

NEGOTIATIONS
are conducted between spouses' lawyers to seek written agreements on as many facts and issues as possible.

MANDATORY MEDIATION
whenever child custody can't be resolved by agreement. Private mediation will usually satisfy this requirement, otherwise you *must* see a court counselor. Court *may* also require an investigation and report on the parties.

PRE–TRIAL SETTLEMENT CONFERENCE
an informal meeting with lawyers, clients, and a judge who will (1) give an opinion on how a trial judge is likely to rule, and (2) try to persuade the parties to settle without trial.

TRIAL

JUDGMENT
and court orders

UNCONTESTED CASES

FILE PETITION
& other legal papers

SERVE SPOUSE
with notice of lawsuit

**OPTIONAL
MARITAL SETTLEMENT
AGREEMENT**
is recommended in cases with a lot of property or maybe if you have children.

JUDGMENT
and court orders

The *disadvantages* to a legal contest, however, are *very* impressive:

- Both sides get drained financially and emotionally.

- Two lawyers will double the personalities in the case and increase the complexity of every step and communication.

- If you have kids, they can get mauled, perhaps permanently. Any hope for future cooperation and co-parenting is seriously impaired.

- Imposed terms are often not adhered to, so you end up in more wrangles, spending more money and time on enforcement.

- Your upset becomes entrenched, runs deeper and lasts longer. Since your real goal is to get on with your life, this holds you back and down—perhaps forever.

Chapter 10 discusses how you can run a controlled battle efficiently, effectively, and avoid some of the worst disadvantages.

Any contested case can become uncontested if one spouse simply drops out of the contest or if the spouses reach an agreement—the earlier the cheaper. However, for a case to drag on and on and not settle until the last minute is *extremely* common and costs almost as much as going to trial. It is not unusual to go to court a number of times, ready for trial, only to have the case continued on one pretext or another. Delays can be caused by crowded courts, or you may be told that delays are used to test the other side, to put pressure on them. But brinksmanship can also be caused by attorneys juggling too many cases and using delay as a disguise for sloppy or inefficient practice.

Our system of justice is known as "the adversary system." It has its historical origins on the medieval field of honor where trial by combat meant that two disputants would battle before a sovereign or other observers and whoever survived was "right." We see some of the same principles and attitudes in our courtrooms today. It is widely believed that the adversary system is a poor forum for settling marital disputes as it tends to increase conflict and does little or nothing to resolve real-life issues.

THE LAWS: There's an old saying: nothing is so simple that it can't be made more complicated if you think about it long enough. Divorce laws have been thought about intensely for generations by thousands of legislators, lawyers, judges, professors, and bureaucrats. Guess what? Our laws are *very* complicated, very hard to read and understand, and constantly changing. This has two obvious disadvantages:

• It is very difficult for the average citizen to understand and use the laws. No ordinary person can possibly keep up with them or understand fully the rules that govern his or her own life. It is absolutely not like that in, say, Texas, where the family laws rarely change and are relatively clear and easy to read. But that doesn't help us in California.

• The volume and complexity of the laws make it easy for any lawyer to complicate any case; in fact, it is sometimes hard for them not to. If a spouse feels like fighting, it is no trouble to find legal issues to fight about.

On the other hand, there is at least one very important advantage to this situation:

• The intricate detail of the laws means that, in most cases, once you have all the facts the outcome is highly predictable. Assuming you don't run afoul of the second item above, this makes it much easier for spouses to settle than it is in states where no one knows what will happen in court.

THE JUDGE used to be a lawyer and was appointed to the bench as a result of political favor (usually) or popular election (occasionally). He or she has an incredible work load and an almost unbearable responsibility to administer cases and do justice. The judge is expected to master a wide variety of intricate legal subjects and be completely current on a frightening volume of cases and statutes that are constantly changing, not to mention the local rules of practice. It is a demanding, almost impossible job. Have pity for the judge.

Courts are typically overbooked and behind. Unless tied up in a trial, most judges will hear a large number of brief matters every day. When not bulldozing through short matters, the process tends to bog down and drag interminably. Delays are typical. Unless you are having a full-blown trial, most of your time in court will be spent waiting, then you will be expected to move briskly. No one wants to hear any more of your story than is absolutely necessary to process your case as quickly as possible. You can't expect to understand very much of what goes on. That's your day in court.

THE LAWYER is a trained combatant for hire. He or she will fight for you—when necessary, before a judge who hears both sides and decides who has told the truth, what the facts are, and how the law applies.

The lawyer's job is to establish the facts of your case, determine how the law applies, use lawyer's techniques to see that you get the most you can, and protect your legal "interests" in property, support, custody and visitation. In a divorce, the lawyer's tools are negotiation (letters and phone calls) and the lawsuit, which involves legal pleadings, motions, and discovery. Discovery is a powerful tool which requires the opposition (your spouse) to deliver copies of documents and to answer questions orally or in writing, under oath, about facts in your marriage. Popular motions include OSCs (orders to show cause) and TROs (temporary restraining orders) which can be used at any time—usually right at the beginning of conflicted cases—to keep the peace, freeze accounts, preserve assets from waste and misuse, and so on.

In spite of popular belief, lawyers are not *always* villains and not *always* to blame for stirring up conflict. Conflict is already lively in most divorces; in fact, lawyers are often more moderate than their clients. But even for well-meaning lawyers, the tools they use and the system they work in will usually increase conflict. Law schools have no course requirements in counseling, family dynamics, or communication skills, and very little if anything on negotiation. Legal training stresses manipulation of complex rules of law, aggressive and defensive strategy, how to take any side of any case and make the most of it, how to argue, how to get the most financial advantage in every situation. Because of their training and professional standards, lawyers tend to threaten, argue, and bully.

In addition to training, professional standards of practice dictate how a lawyer will conduct your case. For example, professional ethics forbid your lawyer to communicate directly with your spouse—the adversary. It is expected, instead, that your spouse will be represented and protected by another lawyer. This means that your attorney will *always* have a one-sided view of your case and can never achieve an objective, independent view or a depth of understanding any greater than your own. Lawyers frequently complain that seeing only one side makes it hard to reach a true understanding of a case.

Here is a little-discussed feature of law practice. In any community, divorce lawyers know each other and can expect to work with or against one another throughout their entire professional careers, so therefore the relationship between opposing counsel will frequently be stronger than between attorney and client. They have their future practice and their professional reputations to think of. Opinions are divided as to whether this is good or bad for the client, and while there's nothing you can do about it, you should know how things stand.

Want to know why escalation and increased conflict is almost certain in an uncontrolled case? Most lawyers start off asking for more than you want or can reasonably expect as a matter of "good" practice. They will routinely file a motion asking for a hearing to get temporary, pre-trial orders for such things as possession of the family home, custody and support until such time as the matter can be heard in full. Then, when your spouse is served with the Petition, it comes with a strong

warning that a Response must be filed within thirty days. When confronted with these imposing documents, an impending court appearance and the need to quickly file a legal response, your spouse is certain to feel threatened and upset. Because you have a lawyer, your spouse is compelled to get a lawyer too. Your spouse's lawyer will oppose your lawyer's exaggerated demands by offering less and by attacking your own case at its weakest points. Now you're off to a good, hot start.

Two attorneys start off costing just double, but pretty soon they begin writing letters, filing motions, taking discovery and doing standard lawyer-type things, just like they were taught and according to professional standards of practice. Now we have a hotly contested case, lots of fees and charges, and a couple of very upset spouses. Fees in contested cases can run from many thousands of dollars *each* all the way up to *everything*.

Lawyers almost always bill by the hour, anything from $80 to $500 per hour, but $150 to $250 is quite common. Why so much? Legal work is inherently inefficient, requiring a lot of time and red tape for minor accomplishments, so the lawyer needs a staff of secretaries and paralegals to do most of the work. Most lawyers maintain an expensive overhead and a rich lifestyle. They "need" a nice office, a classy image, nice cars, meals in good restaurants, and a large library of expensive legal books so they don't have to run to the library. Doing business that way, it really is hard to make ends meet. Billing for every possible moment is the major consideration in almost every practice.

Lawyers sail along like a grand yacht, but they are under enormous pressure to work too hard and run too fast just to keep afloat. They need to juggle a lot of new clients and a large case load just to break even and then add some more to get ahead. Guess who pays?

The high pressure and large case load is part of the reason why lawyers are notorious for dragging cases along, not staying in touch, not answering your calls, not helping you understand your case. Most people who are represented feel out of touch, poorly informed, and helpless. In one study, nearly half of those that were represented said they had fewer than three contacts with their lawyers. Even where there was significant lawyer assistance, contacts were few. About 60% reported they had to work out all issues without the help of their attorneys.

Later, you will learn how to avoid lawyers when possible and how to use them in the most efficient manner, for specific information, advice and tasks. You will learn how to keep the bills down even in a contested case.

Three main messages

Drawn from the last chapters, there are three messages about the legal divorce that are worth emphasizing. It is very important for you to understand that:

One: The legal divorce is limited and narrow in its scope. Apart from the important symbolic value of legal action and legally dissolving the bonds of matrimony, what the legal divorce deals with is peace, property, custody and support. What you get are findings of facts and orders on those subjects. The legal divorce alone rarely solves emotional or life-problems and often cannot even solve practical ones. In fact, when done in the usual way, legal action is all too likely to stimulate conflict and upset.

Two: In most cases, the outcome of legal action on most issues is highly predictable. Once the facts are established, an experienced attorney who knows the laws and the local judges can make very good predictions about what the outcome of legal action will be. There is usually very little to gain from legal battle —in most cases your fees and costs will far exceed anything you could win from fighting your case in court.

Three: The worst possible thing you can do is to simply go find a lawyer and ask for a divorce. It is important—and easy—to take another path. What you want to do is learn about divorce and take control of your own case. That's what the rest of this book is about.

7

Get Organized

Getting information is the best thing you can do to get a better divorce; the next most important thing is being prepared. This means preparing yourself and preparing your case.

Preparing your case means getting the facts of your case clear and organized. The first three of the four worksheets at the end of this chapter are exactly what a good attorney would want to see. Using them will help you to get your mind and your information in order; it will help you to understand your own case and to pinpoint exactly where more information or advice is necessary. If you prepare your case with these worksheets and gather supporting documents before you visit an attorney, you will start off saving hours of time and many hundreds of dollars. You will impress the attorney as being well informed and prepared—someone who knows what they are doing.

Preparing yourself includes getting information about divorce, just as you have been doing by reading this book. The real-life issues of the real divorce can be very hard to work out and may take a long time to clarify. But in the legal divorce, the issues are much more specific—what do you want to do about property, custody and support? First, you start by learning how divorce works and how the laws apply to your case. Then, when necessary, you find out the likely outcome given the facts in your case. After that, the final step of preparation is to decide what you want.

Decide what you want

Deciding what you want requires an understanding of what you have a right to under the law (what you are likely to get in court) and what your life priorities are. Think about what is important to you: security, property, money, revenge, income, peace of mind, your children, cooperative co-parenting, future relationship, doing what's right, being fair, forgiveness, and so on. Then think about what is the most important. Attorneys generally work on the premise that getting the most you can is what is important, but you may have different values. You may prefer your values to the legal ones. Getting every last cent may not be as important to you as other things. Or maybe it is.

Spend some time with the worksheets. Start working on them *right now,* today. Once you have done as much as you can, make a list of any questions you have and additional information you need. Start making a list of the issues in your case and the things you need to decide. You probably won't have any difficulty, but if you do have trouble reaching conclusions or if you are not confident about it, the time has come to seek advice. At least you have pin-pointed exactly what you need to know. Now you can go to an attorney and ask some very specific questions and get some very specific advice. Do that, then think things over and decide what you want. But make up your own mind—don't live on someone else's values.

Don't give away too much out of fear, guilt, or a desire to have it done with faster; you'll only feel bad about it later. Don't be guided by a desire for revenge—it's too expensive. Don't force a legal battle over small issues or for marginal gains. Be fair to yourself, then be fair to your spouse.

Fill out the worksheets

At the end of this chapter you will find four worksheets that will help you organize and analyze your case. The pages are perforated, so you can tear them out.

General instructions for all worksheets

• Make one copy of the blanks forms before you fill them out so you can have a rough draft, then a final copy. Duplicate your final copy whenever you need to give a copy to a professional helping you with your case.

• Put N/A in spaces where the information requested is not applicable to your situation, or put a line through the entire section if it is not relevant; this is so a reader will know that you did not simply forget the item. Put EST where an amount is estimated.

• Pencil in UNK where you don't know the requested information. Keep a list of things you don't yet know. There may be some things you can't find out, but put some effort into digging out information and completing as much of the forms as possible.

• If you run out of room on any item, attach another sheet, put down "continuation of item ___," and continue. When you are completely finished, note the total number of additional pages at the top of the first sheet on the line provided and staple them all together.

The Personal Information Worksheet

This worksheet and the next are adapted from client intake forms used in the family law practice of Barbara Di Franza of Di Franza & Portman in San Jose, California. The first one is quite straightforward and fairly self-evident. It is important and useful in any kind of case and should be filled out by everyone.

Although gathering facts can be tedious work, it is an extremely useful thing you can do and it will save you a lot of money if you do it yourself. However, there are two situations where you may want professional help: 1) if your estate is large or complex—if, for example, you own an on-going business—you may want to consult an accountant or an attorney; and 2) if you think your mate may be hiding information, documents or assets, then you will want to consult an attorney about getting the facts under oath.

Notes:

• Items 11, 12, 22, and 23: information about former names is primarily for women who want to take this easy opportunity to have their name legally changed to their maiden name or to a former married name.
• Item 29: if a child does not yet have a social security number, get one. It is important to the enforcement of support orders and necessary for tax exemptions.
• Items 16 and 27 request information on the monetary arrangements with people you and your spouse live with (if any). This is asking if any of the people named are dependents or are otherwise being supported, or if any of them contribute to the household expenses.

THE ASSETS WORKSHEET

If you have any property or bills to divide, you should fill out this worksheet.

Notes:
• You will need to find copies of documents related to any property on this worksheet: deeds, mortgages, trust deeds, notes, registration papers for motor vehicles, serial numbers for major items, account numbers for financial and retirement accounts, and so on. Make copies to hand over if you consult an attorney about your case.
• The value of property is always "fair-market value" which means the amount you can get for the item if sold on the open market less any costs of sale. You will need a professional appraisal for real property, pensions, a going business, or any items of uncertain or disputed value.
• Item 1 (f) and (i) is where you indicate if money for the purchase of the family home came from the separate property of either spouse.

future. It can serve as a basis for your discussions on how co-parenting can work.

Go over all the items and indicate with M and F who does what and how often. To be very thorough, estimate the number of hours actually spent per month on each activity and put that number next to each entry in the left column, then add it all up. In the right column, estimate how child-care will work under whatever co-parenting terms are under consideration.

Decisions: Will custody be shared? If not, who will have physical custody and primary responsibility? If one parent gets physical custody, how can parenting be arranged so each parent gets maximum time with the children?

Parenting plans and visitation: In most cases it is best to have your future parenting schedule spelled out in as much detail as possible so everyone knows exactly what to expect and so there are no arguments later. In actual practice, parents can always agree to any arrangements they like at the time, but whenever there are disagreements, a detailed, specific schedule will settle the matter and save a lot of disagreement in the future. Any plan you make can always can always be changed when you are both in a co-operative mood.

Keep good records

Your work will be easier and go smoother if you are careful to keep your records safe, neat, organized, and all together in one place. Otherwise, you may end up swamped in a mass of papers that will only stimulate your feeling of confusion and frustration. You might misplace important papers. It's easier if you start off right.

Keep file folders in a drawer or box, or go to a stationers and get a large accordion folder with six or more compartments, or just use some large envelopes in a box. Keep a set of files for:

- Correspondence with
  - lawyers
  - spouse
  - others
- Legal Pleadings
- Other Documents
- Worksheets
- Any other categories that will help you sort things out.

Personal information in the marriage of _____

_____
date

There are _____ additional pages attached to this worksheet

ABOUT THE MARRIAGE

1. Date of marriage: _____   Place of marriage: _____
   city   state

2. Date of separation: _____
   (when one of us left the marital bed or at least clearly said the marriage was over)

3. I have resided in California for _____ years and in the County of _____ for _____ years.
   My spouse resided in Calif. for _____ years and in the County of _____ for _____ years.

4. The divorce is desired by: ___Husband   ___Wife

5. There are _____ children born or adopted into this marriage (further information below)

6. Description of any acts of harassment or violence:

   _____
   _____
   _____
   _____

ABOUT MYSELF

7. Name: _____

8. Telephones: Home: (_____) _____
                    Work: (_____) _____   OK to phone at work? _____
                    Other: (_____) _____   OK to leave message? _____

9. Sex: _____   Age: _____   Date of birth: _____

10. Mailing address: _____
    street   city   state   zip
    Residence address: _____

    County of residence: _____   How long? _____

11. Former name(s): _____

12. ___I do not wish a former name restored.
    ___I want my former name restored as follows: _____

13. Employer:_____

    Address: _____
                    street   city   state   zip
    Days and times at work: _____

    Length of this employment:_____ Approximate monthly gross pay: $_____

    There is medical / dental coverage through my employer:

            _____ for me _____for my spouse _____for children Monthly cost: $_____

    My Social Security number:_____

    Cost of child care enabling me to work is $_____ per month.

14. Other sources of income: Approx. amount per month:
    a)_____   _____
    b)_____   _____
    c)_____   _____

15. Health problems for which special attention or care is necessary:
    _____
    _____

16. Other than my spouse or children, I am currently residing with:

Name	Age	Relationship to me
_____	_____	_____
_____	_____	_____
_____	_____	_____

    Monetary arrangements: _____
    _____

17. ___I have no will.   ___My most recent will was made on_____.

ABOUT MY SPOUSE

18. Name: _____

19. Telephones: Home: (____)_____
                       Work: (____)_____ OK to phone at work?_____
                       Other: (____)_____ OK to leave message?_____

20. Sex: _____   Age:_____   Date of birth: _____

21. Mailing address:_____
                          street   city   state   zip
    Residence address:_____

    County of residence:_____   How long?_____

22. Former name(s): _____

23. ___Spouse does not wish a former name restored.
    ___Spouse wants former name restored as follows:_____

24. Employer:_____

    Address: _____
                          street   city   state   zip
    Days and times at work: _____

    Length of this employment:_____   Approximate monthly gross pay: $_____

    There is medical / dental coverage through spouse's employer:

          _____ for me   _____for my spouse   _____for children   Monthly cost: $_____

    Spouse's Social Security number:_____

    Cost of child care enabling spouse to work is $_____ per month.

25. Other sources of income: Approx. amount per month:
    a)_____   _____
    b)_____   _____
    c)_____   _____

26. Health problems for which special attention or care is necessary:
    _____
    _____

27. Other than our children, my spouse currently resides with:

       Name   Age   Relationship to spouse

    _____   ____   _____
    _____   ____   _____
    _____   ____   _____
    _____   ____   _____

    Monetary arrangements with the above persons (known) (suspected):_____
    _____

28. Spouse's attorney is:_____
       Address:_____

CHILDREN BORN OR ADOPTED INTO THIS MARRIAGE

29.　　　　　Name　　　　　　　　　Age　　Birth date　　Soc. Sec. #　　Residing with

_____　___　_____　_____　_____
_____　___　_____　_____　_____
_____　___　_____　_____　_____
_____　___　_____　_____　_____

There (is) (is not) likely to be any dispute about the paternity of any of the children.

30. Special health care problems:_____
_____
_____

31. Income or property owned by any dependent children:
_____
_____
_____

32. Custody and visitation of children:
　　　a) is currently arranged and is working out as follows:

_____
_____
_____
_____

　　　b) I want the judgment to order custody and visitation rights as follows:

_____
_____
_____
_____

　　　c) I anticipate that there (will) (will not) be a dispute over custody and visitation.

MY PREVIOUS MARRIAGES & RELATIONSHIPS

33. I was previously married ____ times before this marriage.

　　　Name of my former spouse(s)　　　　　　　When terminated　　How (death, divorce, etc.)
a)_____　　_____　　_____
b)_____　　_____　　_____
c)_____　　_____　　_____

34. Children born or adopted into the previous marriage(s):
　　　　　Name　　　　　　　　　　　Age　　Birth date　　Residing with

_____　___　_____　_____
_____　___　_____　_____
_____　___　_____　_____

35. Children from a non-marital relationship:

Name	Age	Birth date	Residing with
_____	_____	_____	_____
_____	_____	_____	_____

36. Support paid or received (including any overdue) by me or by the above children, or other income (such as Social Security) received by or on behalf of the above children, is as follows:

_____

_____

_____

_____

MY SPOUSE'S PREVIOUS MARRIAGES & RELATIONSHIPS

37. My spouse was previously married ____ times before this marriage.

Name of former spouse	When terminated	How (death, divorce, etc.)
a)_____	_____	_____
b)_____	_____	_____
c)_____	_____	_____

38. My spouse's children born or adopted into the previous marriage(s):

Name	Age	Birth date	Residing with
_____	_____	_____	_____
_____	_____	_____	_____
_____	_____	_____	_____

39. My spouse's children from a non-marital relationship:

Name	Age	Birth date	Residing with
_____	_____	_____	_____
_____	_____	_____	_____
_____	_____	_____	_____

40. Support paid or received (including any overdue) by my spouse or by the above children, or other income (such as Social Security) received by or on behalf of the above children, is as follows:

_____

_____

_____

CURRENT ARRANGEMENTS

41. ___We are not yet separated
___We are separated but have no financial arrangements at this time.
___We have separated and now live apart under the following financial arrangements:

Periodic payments (who pays, how much, for what, how often): _____
_____
_____

Direct payments (Mortgage, bills, et cetera.)

Who pays?	Item	amount	how often paid

Other arrangements: _____
_____
_____

42. ___We have made no written agreements and have no oral understandings.
___We have a written agreement which is attached.
___We have oral agreements or understandings as follows: _____
_____
_____
_____
_____

PENDING ISSUES AND QUESTIONS

43. I foresee the following problems in dealing with my spouse (i.e., fear, distrust, dishonesty, unwillingness to compromise, using children as a weapon, violence, et cetera): _____
_____
_____
_____
_____

44. I have some questions and issues I would like to explore, as follows: _____
_____
_____
_____
_____

45. I have already made some decisions about what outcome I would like with respect to property, children, support, or goals and conduct of this case, as follows: _____
_____
_____
_____
_____

Assets in the marriage of _____

Date _____

There are _____ additional pages attached to this worksheet

1. The family home

___We do not own and are not buying the family home (skip to 2.)
___We own or are buying the family home, with an approximate market value of $_____

a) Address:_____
        street   city   county   state

b) Date of original purchase:_____

c) Title is now in name of ___Husband ___Wife Other: _____

d) Title is held as ___Joint Tenants ___Tenants in Common ___Community Property
    ___Other: _____

    ___Title has been changed since we first acquired it as described here: _____
    _____
    _____

e) ___We both agree that the house should be divided:
        ___50/50 ___Other: _____

    ___We disagree about the division of the house as follows: _____
        _____
        _____

    ___There have been ___oral ___written understandings or agreements about ownership of the
        family home, or about reimbursement for money spent on purchase or improvements (give dates,
        and details):_____
        _____

f) The money for the down payment of $ _____ was provided by:
                                    Amount   Source of funds (indicate if separate property used)
    ___Our joint savings _____   _____
    ___Husband _____   _____
    ___Wife _____   _____
    ___Other _____   _____

g) Money borrowed when home was first purchased:
                            Amount   Original Balance   Current Balance
    (1) First Deed of Trust _____   _____   _____
    (2) Second Deed of Trust _____   _____   _____

    Later Deeds of Trust _____   _____   _____

h) __The home was never refinanced.   __The home was refinanced on (date):_____
i) House payments during the marriage were made:
    __entirely from the wages of either spouse.
    __other, as follows (include payments from separate property of either spouse):_____
_____

2   Other real estate

__Neither spouse owns or is buying any other real estate (skip to 3).
__I or my spouse own the following types of other real estate.
    (Type: R = rental, U = unimproved land, F = farm or ranch, C = commercial property)

	Type	Address	Date purchased	Purchase price	Current Value
a)					
b)					
c)					
d)					

	Amount & source of down pmt.	Balance owed on property	Title in name of H, W, Other	Amount of + or - cash flow per month
a)				
b)				
c)				
d)				

3. Automobiles

	Registered to	Year	Make	Model	Amount owed	Approx. Miles	Value
a)							
b)							
c)							
d)							

4. Personal property:
Identify items of special monetary or sentimental value, then lump the rest into general categories such as furniture, appliances, tools, garden equipment, hobby equipment, books, records, sports equipment, paintings, et cetera.

	Description	Value	Amount owing	Who owns it? (H, W, both, other)
a)				
b)				
c)				
d)				
e)				
f)				
g)				
h)				
i)				
j)				
k)				
l)				
m)				
n)				

5. Cash accounts (Checking, saving, credit union, money market, T-bills, certificates of deposit)

In name of H, W, Other	Where held, Type of Acct.	Balance at separation	Balance now	Maturity date	Who controls it? H, W, Other
a)					
b)					
c)					
d)					
e)					

6. Retirement accounts (IRA or Keogh) held by either spouse

In name of H, W, Other	Institution and Branch	Type of Account	Approximate value/ amount	Maturity date
a)				
b)				
c)				
d)				

7. Securities (Mutual funds, bonds, limited partnerships, stocks) owned by either spouse

In name of H, W, Other	Broker (if applicable)	Description (include # of shares, % interest at separation)	Approximate net value
a)			
b)			
c)			
d)			

8. Life insurance policies on either spouse or children

Company	Policy #	Whole or term?	Face Value	Cash value	Beneficiary	Insured
a)						
b)						
c)						
d)						

9. Pension, retirement or profit-sharing benefits in which either spouse *may* have an interest

In name of H or W	Company or Union	Location	Years in plan	Description, amount of benefits
a)				
b)				
c)				
d)				

10. Business interests. Describe any interest held by either spouse in any business, professional practice or corporation, giving approximate value of interest where possible.

_____

_____

_____

_____

_____

11. Tax returns

The last year for which we filed a joint return was _____.

There ____ is no tax refund currently due

____ is still a refund due, $ _____ from the state, $ _____ from the federal government.

Monies owed for previous returns or for returns due to be filed in the next year are as follows: _____

_____

_____

12. Debts

	Creditor	Purpose	Balance at separation	Balance today
a)				
b)				
c)				
d)				
e)				

	Part of debt incurred during marriage, before sep.	Annual interest rate	Monthly payment	Written agreement?	Who has records?
a)					
b)					
c)					
d)					
e)					

13. Education & training:
If community funds were used for education or training of either spouse that substantially increased that spouse's earning capacity, indicate who for and how much. _____

_____

_____

14. Separate property

a) If any of the property listed above is separate, make a note in the left-hand margin — "HS" for Husband's separate property, "WS" for Wife's separate property.

b) List below any other property or debt not listed above that you think is the separate property of either spouse.

	Description	How was it acquired	Whose is it?
a)			
b)			
c)			
d)			
e)			
f)			

c) Note here community funds or property lost due to gambling. Give dates, amounts, and who lost it.

_____

_____

_____

Budget of _____ **Dated** _____

I N C O M E

These figures are *gross* earnings per *month*.
Earnings received on other periods are pro-rated to a monthly figure.

	my income	my spouse's income
EARNINGS		
Salary and wages	$	$
Commissions		
INVESTMENT INCOME		
Interest from savings		
Interest from other accounts		
Dividends		
Rental income (gross income less cash expenses; attach schedule)		
Royalties		
OTHER INCOME		
Business profits		
Pensions		
Trusts		
From retirement accounts (IRA, KEOGH)		
Social Security		
Disability & unemployment		
Spousal Support		
Child Support		
Welfare		
Contributions from live-in mates		
Other:		
TOTAL GROSS INCOME	$	$

DEDUCTIONS FROM GROSS INCOME:

State income tax		
Federal income tax		
Social Security or self-employment tax		
Health insurance		
State disability insurance		
Mandatory pension or retirement deductions		
Mandatory union dues		
Other: (specify)		
TOTAL DEDUCTIONS	$	$
NET SPENDING INCOME (Gross less total deductions)	$	$

E X P E N S E S

Expenses are per month.
Payments on other periods are pro-rated to a monthly figure.

FIXED EXPENSES

	our past joint expenses	my future expenses	spouse's future expenses
1. Household			
Rent or mortgage	$	$	$
Property tax			
Telephone			
Gas & Electric			
Water			
Fuel			
Garbage service			
Cable TV			
Other			
Sub total	$	$	$
2 Taxes			
Federal income tax (beyond pg. 1)	$	$	$
State income tax (beyond pg. 1)			
Sub total	$	$	$
3. Insurance			
Life	$	$	$
Health & accident			
Hospitalization			
Fire & Theft			
Personal Property			
Sub total	$	$	$
4. Payments on debts			
Furniture	$	$	$
Appliances			
Charge accounts			
Credit cards			
Personal loans			
Christmas / Chanukkah club			
Other			
Other			
Sub total	$	$	$

	our past joint expenses	my future expenses	spouse's future expenses

5.   Education for self & kids
Tuition
Room & board
Books
Other

	$	$	$
Sub total	$	$	$

6.   Transportation
Auto payments
Auto insurance
Auto license
Parking
Commuting to work
Other

	$	$	$
Sub total	$	$	$

7.   Personal allowance
Self
Child(ren)
Music lessons
Support for parents
Other dependents

	$	$	$
Sub total	$	$	$

8.   Memberships
Union (beyond amount on page 1)
Professional associations
Clubs
Religious
Other

	$	$	$
Sub total	$	$	$

Total fixed expenses	$	$	$

FLEXIBLE EXPENSES

9.   Food
Groceries
Meals out (includes school lunches)

	$	$	$
Sub total	$	$	$

	our past joint expenses	my future expenses	spouse's future expenses

10. Household expenses

Cleaning materials $ $ $
Small home items
Yard care
House cleaning
House maintenance
Repairs
New appliances
New furniture
Home improvements

    Sub total $ $ $

11. Clothing

New clothes
  Self $ $ $
  Children
Laundry
Dry cleaning
Repairs

    Sub total $ $ $

12. Transportation

Gas & oil $ $ $
Auto repair & upkeep
Non-commuting bus or train fares

    Sub total $ $ $

13. Health (not covered by insurance)

Medical $ $ $
Dental
Drugs & medication
Other

    Sub total $ $ $

14. Personal

Grooming supplies $ $ $
Barber or beauty services
Snacks
Theater & movies
Baby sitter
Hobbies
Vacation

	our past joint expenses	my future expenses	spouse's future expenses
Magazines	$	$	$
Newspapers			
Stationary & postage			
Alcohol			
Tobacco			
Home entertainment			
Other	_____	_____	_____
Sub total	$	$	$

15. Gifts (beyond the Christmas/Chanukkah funds, above)

	our past joint expenses	my future expenses	spouse's future expenses
Christmas/Chanukkah	$	$	$
Birthdays			
Weddings			
Religious celebrations			
Anniversaries			
Other	_____	_____	_____
Sub total	$	$	$

16. Contributions

	our past joint expenses	my future expenses	spouse's future expenses
Religious	$	$	$
Charity			
Schools / colleges			
Other	_____	_____	_____
Sub total	$	$	$
Total flexible expenses	$	$	$
TOTAL EXPENSES	$	$	$

There are _____ additional pages attached to this worksheet

Parental Activity Worksheet

for_____

Enter an M *and* an F for each item to show activity of *both* mother and father
Optional: Estimate time spent per month by each parent on each item

	Past Experience					Future Plans				
	always	usually	equally	seldom	never	always	usually	equally	seldom	never
Change diapers										
Buy clothes										
Cut hair										
Do laundry										
Wash hair										
Make breakfast										
Make lunch										
Make dinner										
Pack lunch, lunch money										
Consult with teachers										
Answer birthday invitations										
Teach to throw ball										
Play										
Read stories										
Buy gifts for parties										
Buy groceries										
Do dishes										
Fill out school papers										
Help with homework										
Arrange for sitters										
Put to bed										
Teach manners										
Teach problem solving										
Make brush teeth										
Arrange birthday parties										
Take trick or treating										
Make bed										
Fold and put away clothes										
Set TV and play rules										
Tend to minor hurts										
Take to doctor for checkup										
Take to dentist										
Tend when sick										
Maintain medical records										
Take to school first day										
Discipline										

	Past Experience					Future Plans				
	always	usually	equally	seldom	never	always	usually	equally	seldom	never
Mend clothes										
Maintain toys										
Teach to clean up										
Pack for trips										
Take to outside lessons										
Take to visit child's friends										
Arrange for friends to come										
Take to Sunday school, church										
Take to sport activities										
Take out to play										
Attend PTA meetings										
Choose best schools, classes										

Others (be specific):

GET GOING 1: THE SMOOTH ROAD
—cases with no legal opposition

You should read this chapter, no matter how much conflict there might be in your case. It will help you understand some advantages of an unopposed case and what happens after you *do* finally reach an agreement.

This chapter is about dealing with the legal divorce in cases where you do not expect your spouse to oppose you legally. Maybe your spouse is long gone, or doesn't care, or there isn't enough at stake to fight about, or you completely agree already, or he or she just isn't the type of person who would go to a lawyer and struggle and squabble....or whatever.

Unopposed cases are so simple to do, you may well wonder why lawyers charge so much for just filling out some forms. There are two reasons. First, most people who go to lawyers for a divorce are uninformed and unprepared, so the lawyer has to spend time hand–holding, listening to a lot of emotional blow–off, and waiting for clients to figure out what they want to do. Second, and perhaps more significant, lawyers have a monopoly. If you want a lawyer, you have to pay the price. After reading this book, you will know that there are many advantages to limiting or eliminating the lawyer's role, especially in an unopposed case. You will find that you have some very good alternatives and that you can get along just fine with very little, if any, of a lawyer's time.

In getting through the *legal* part of an unopposed case, the only difficult part is having to make decisions—what to do about your community property, your kids, and support arrangements, if any. It is very important for you to understand and decide these things for yourself anyway, whether you use a lawyer or not.

How to keep an easy case easy: Many cases start out unopposed, but sometimes an unopposed case can blow up into conflict. Fortunately, that's something you can learn to avoid, although it isn't necessarily easy to do. The techniques you use to deal with flare–ups are the same ones you use to quiet and settle a case that starts out conflicted. This is covered in Chapter 9 where we discuss how to reduce conflict and how to negotiate terms.

Be sure your spouse has a copy of this book. Give one to him or her if necessary—it can only help. That way, you will *both* have good information and maybe you can talk about ideas and solutions suggested here.

Making decisions

In unopposed cases, how easy it will be for you to understand your case and make sound decisions about your divorce—about your own life, after all—will depend entirely on things like:
* how complex the facts of your case are,
* your level of self–confidence,
* how much initiative you can muster, and
* how emotionally wrought up you are.

Notice that only the first factor is objective—about conditions and events "out there." Everything else depends on your own attitude and your emotional condition.

Getting your hands on the nuts and bolts of your own divorce may appear to be difficult or tedious to some people—something they would rather avoid—but it is *very* important for you to do it. Making life decisions is not something you can safely or wisely leave to any other person. Besides, the rewards for dealing with it yourself far outweigh the effort. Dealing with your own affairs is practical, constructive, useful work. It helps you to organize your mind and your experience. It saves you a pile of money and loads of aggravation. It feels good to be in charge of your own life. It is the best way to get the best possible outcome in your case and it gives you an excellent start on your independent new life. Okay, when the whistle sounds.......go!

You have to decide 1) how to divide your community property; 2) how to arrange for the shared parenting of kids, if you have any; and 3) how much support, if any, will be provided for a spouse or children. Maybe your case is very simple or maybe you are already clear about what you want and what's fair. If so, just go right ahead. But in most cases you will want to learn more about what the law would do in your case before you make any final decisions.

Try to avoid making long–term decisions when you are in the shock or rollercoaster stages of your divorce. Don't build the rest of your life on decisions based on anger, guilt or expediency. Be careful that you don't give away too much out of fear, guilt, or just to get it over with. People who do this often regret it later. Be equally careful not to pressure your spouse with guilt or fear. Experience shows that this kind of thing is very likely to backfire later.

If you are numb, emotionally wrought up or under extreme stress, slow things way down—stop for a while if you can arrange it. Try to put off making permanent decisions until you are on a more even keel. Try to create short–term, temporary solutions instead of long–term, permanent ones. If you can't put off making permanent decisions until things settle down, then you should be very strongly guided by the rules of law. Consider getting independent advice before you make any final agreements or decisions.

Remember that it is possible to separate the gathering of information from the making of decisions. Once you have information about the rules and the likely outcome of your case under the rules, then if you still have trouble making decisions, you can use a marriage counselor to help you decide as well as an attorney, or you can call us at Divorce Help Line (1-800-359-7004). The choice depends on the nature of your problems and on your personal preference. Making life decisions is really more of a personal than a legal issue. How to choose a counselor is discussed in Chapter 9.

Whenever you are in doubt about what you want or what is right, let the legal standards be your guide. They can save you from common mistakes, like giving up too much and regretting it when it's too late, or demanding more than you can expect to win. The laws have been worked out over many decades and millions of cases, so should not be disregarded lightly. On the other hand, you don't need to guide your life according to the law if you have other values that are strong, clear and important to you. The law is meant to settle contested cases where the judge has to decide things according to the rules, but spouses can settle their affairs almost

any way they like. However, judges *will* carefully examine terms concerning children to be sure the kids are being properly supported and protected, but will otherwise give you your way in most cases.

Learning more about the rules: In some cases, to make decisions may require that you find out more about the laws on a certain subject and how they apply to the facts of your case. Have a look at the end of Chapter 5 where we discussed four good ways to learn more about the law.

Marital settlement agreements

You should think seriously about making a written agreement whenever your spouse is in the picture and you can agree about how you want to handle the legal issues in your divorce.

Consider the advantages:
- Getting a written agreement ties things down, gives you clarity and a record of exactly what you agreed to—in case misunderstandings come up later.
- When you file your Petition, it will help your spouse feel better about letting the divorce go through without contest or representation since the terms of the judgment are all settled.
- The judge will be reassured that the terms are agreeable to both spouses. This is especially important if you are seeking anything at all out of the ordinary.
- People who make written agreements are far more likely to comply with the terms than when the same terms are imposed on them.
- It usually leads to better post–divorce relationship with your ex–spouse. This is especially important if you have children.

A written agreement is especially important when you have property that is valuable or sentimentally important to you and worth some effort to protect. You can clarify which items are separate, which are community, and how the community property is to be divided.

If you have children, you may want to work out terms for custody, visiting and other co–parenting issues. You can, of course, informally depart from your own terms at your mutual convenience, but at least you will have worked out what your minimum mutual expectations are about co–parenting.

You can examine a typical, simple marital settlement agreement in *How To Do Your Own Divorce* and use it as a guide for making your own agreement. You can also work out your basic terms, then hire an attorney just to draw up your agreement, then handle everything else yourself. You can also call Divorce Help Line (1-800-359-7004) for information, advice, or assistance.

How to get your divorce

Each year, between 35,000 and 55,000 California divorces are done successfully without much help from lawyers, and the number might easily be much higher. There are three ways this happens:

• **Do-it-yourself:** Most people start by getting the book, *How To Do Your Own Divorce*, and then decide if they want to do the whole thing themselves. Unopposed divorces are so easy that at least 500,000 people in California have done their own divorces with cases at every level of complexity, saving thousands of dollars for *each spouse*. This is the least expensive way to get a divorce.

• **Divorce typing services:** The second way lawyerless divorces get done is with the help of a divorce typing service. Their fees average about $200 plus costs and filing fees. The theory is that you know what you want and merely hire secretarial assistance for the tedious job of preparing and filing your forms. These people are not usually trained in law or counseling, so it is important that you be informed and know exactly what you want when you use a divorce typing service.

There are probably over 100 divorce typing services in California. Most of them keep a notice running in the personal classified section of their local newspapers. This kind of service has existed since 1973 with *relatively* few reported problems. But, still, you should be careful when you choose one to work with. Before you hire someone, find out how long they have been in business, talk to them, talk to people they have worked with, and make up your own mind. This alternative service is safest and works best when you are informed and prepared. Then you know what's going on and can supervise their work and progress—same as with a lawyer.

   • **Divorce Help Line:** The third way you can get your own divorce is with assistance from Divorce Help Line (1-800-359-7004). DHL has a staff of expert attorneys and paralegals with no other purpose than to help you get through your divorce the best and least expensive way possible. It costs a bit more than the independent paralegal service, but the training and experience of the staff is the best in California. They can answer your questions, give legal advice and counseling, and do all or part of your paperwork for you. See page one for more information, and call for a rate quote.

If anyone offers to sell you a fast, cheap divorce from the Dominican Republic, or anywhere else outside of California, and if they say you don't have to live there or go to a hearing, you are probably in the presence of a person who is ignorant or unscrupulous or both. Don't do it! Foreign divorces that can be bought without either spouse going there are not worth the price of the paper. If you want to be a good citizen and help prevent others from being taken, call your county District Attorney and file a report.

You may, of course, decide to have a lawyer handle your divorce from start to finish. Many people still do. This costs a *lot* more but may be necessary in cases with unavoidable conflict or a very high degree of complexity. You should probably hire a certified family law specialist. Read Chapter 11 about choosing and using a lawyer.

There are cheap lawyers who run divorce mills, but here, as anywhere, you frequently get what you pay for. If they do not complicate your case and promote more legal work for themselves, they will essentially be doing the work of a divorce typist for a much higher price. Cheap lawyers can't take the time to help you understand your case; they are notorious for not returning your calls. If they get into a conflict with a well-paid attorney, they can't keep up the same level of attention and will be working your case at a disadvantage.

If you go the lawyer route, take care that lawyerly techniques do not increase the conflict or complexity of your case, and that you do not get more legal action than you really need. Be prepared, know what's going on, supervise and manage your own case. That's what works best.

GET GOING 2: THE ROCKY ROAD
—cases with opposition and conflict

This chapter is about how to deal with divorce in cases where the spouses are in active disagreement—including the whole range from simple difference of opinion to active upset and anger, all the way to outright violence.

You should know that the vast majority of all cases are settled before they get to trial. Only about 10% of all California divorces are actually fought out in court, so you can see that *your* case is *very* likely to settle sooner or later. Unfortunately, although most divorces settle, many do so only after the spouses have spent their emotional energies on conflict and their financial resources on lawyers, so when the ashes settle the spouses get to divide whatever is left over—their share of the ashes. The time and effort spent battling has impaired their ability to get on with their lives and may have caused serious psychic damage to themselves and their children.

The ironic thing is that the outcomes of most cases are relatively predictable from the beginning, so the spouses could have saved themselves a lot of financial waste and emotional anguish by agreeing to settle before the big battle. Why didn't they? Failure to reach agreement is usually caused by a high degree of emotional upset, the fear and anger common to most divorces. Complex and volatile emotions become externalized; they get attached to things or to your children. When emotions are high, reason is at its lowest ebb and will not be very effective at *that time*.

This chapter is about how you can deal with conflict and how to reduce it to reach an agreement. The next chapter is about what to do if you don't want to or can't agree. We are addressing a very wide range of possible situations here, so just use whatever seems useful in your own situation.

How to deal with extreme conflict

Is your spouse violent? Alcoholic? A *terrible* nuisance? In extreme cases of harassment or violence there are legal remedies and there are practical things that you can, and must, do for yourself. This is not about how to reach agreement—these are strategies for self-defense. Mental and physical abuse must never be tolerated.

Automatice restraining orders: The legal remedy for harassment and domestic violence is to get a restraining order—a document from the court, served personally on your spouse, forbidding certain conduct. Every divorce automatically includes a restraining order against physical abuse and harrasment (see Chapter 5—Keeping the peace).

More: In severe cases, where there has been physical harm to you or your children and where future harm is threatened, you can go to court for stronger orders—to have your spouse ordered to get out and stay away from the family residence. Child visitation can be ordered for specific times and places, away from your home, or, in bad cases, under supervision. It takes very clear proof of *extreme* danger or detriment to the child to forbid visitation altogether.

If a divorce action is pending, any effort to get a restraining order must be made a part of your divorce lawsuit. Any way you do it, you file a motion with the court, then have a hearing at which you present evidence and the other party has a chance to be heard. In very extreme cases where there is clear evidence of danger, orders can be issued *ex parte*—without notice to or participation of your spouse—which are binding only until a hearing can be held and more orders issued after hearing both sides. You may want the assistance of an attorney to get restraining orders as part of a divorce action.

When you request temporary orders as part of your divorce action, you can get a wider range of orders. In addition to restraining orders, you can also request temporary orders for support, custody, or visitation that will set the terms of your separation until a full-scale trial is held or a settlement is reached. Temporary orders can be very useful if you need them to stabilize your case or get support coming in.

The real question about restraining orders is this: after you have the orders, how do you enforce them? Will just serving the orders on your spouse make enough of an impression to be effective? If you file your restraining order with the police, they are *required* to try to enforce it, but if your spouse violates the restraining order anyway, you will probably have to take your spouse back to court again. The judge can lecture, threaten, and hold your spouse in contempt for ignoring court orders, and possibly set some jail time (sentence suspended) to be served if bad conduct is repeated. Judges seem, in general, to be getting a bit tougher, but still, only in extreme cases will a spouse actually be locked away, and only very briefly. Then what?

Here's the good news: ninety per-cent of all restraining orders are adhered to. Being served with orders from a court seems to have a psychological effect on most abusers, and, more to the point, they show that you are very serious about not being a victim any longer.

Police: You should be sure to notify the police in any case of serious domestic harassment or violence—but you should also be aware of the practical realities of police intervention.

The police may be an unreliable source of help in domestic situations, although this will vary from place to place. They have been accused of prejudice and sexism, but whether or not that is true, their conduct is also based on years of frustrating and dangerous experience. Police are much more likely to get hurt and less likely to do any real good in domestic disputes than in any other kind of case. This difficult issue has received a great deal of public attention, so police agencies are now required to have written standards on dealing with domestic violence and responding officers must give victims written notice of available community services and legal rights. Some departments have officers specially trained in family crisis intervention. Call your local police, talk to them about your problem and see what their attitude is. Start a record.

One of the real advantages of restraining orders is that they can get you a much better response from law enforcement agencies by putting the police under extra pressure to protect you. But whether you have court orders or not, don't hesitate to call the police if you think it might help, and *keep* calling them. At the very least, you will be building a case and developing evidence.

Self-help and other practical considerations: The success of restraining orders and police intervention depends very much on the kind of person your spouse is and what steps you take to protect yourself. Is your spouse the kind of person that will honor and respect a court order? Will he or she care about the police coming out or being dragged into court and talked to sternly by a judge? Does your spouse have a reputation, money or property to protect? Will your spouse, in the heat of rage or hatred, ignore the threat or reality of police presence?

When all is said and done, the best kind of help is the help you give yourself. Starting with the premise that the only thing you can control in life is your own attitude, actions and reactions, start there. What is your attitude? What part do you play in provocation or in being a victim? Try to learn not to do the kinds of things that set your spouse off. This does *not* mean to give up and roll over, but it does mean learning to express yourself cleanly and not to react or provoke. In most disturbed relationships, there is some pattern of action and reaction behavior that builds to an eruption. Try to understand your part and stop responding to the cues. Don't let yourself get provoked, and when provoked, don't react in kind.

Don't be a victim. Spouse abuse is a *very* common problem so you are not unique or alone. Nearly every community has professionals, agencies, and family support groups that have a lot of special knowledge and experience with domestic conflict. They can probably help you. To find a local support group, call your county Superior Court; ask for the Conciliation Court service and ask them for a reference to a local spouse abuse support group. You can also call the California Self-Help Center at 1–800–222-5465 and they

will give you a reference. If one group isn't what you want, try another. Maybe you can get help from friends and family, have someone move in with you for a while, get a roommate (a big one). One obvious practical solution is to move away, at least until things cool down, if not for good. Change all the locks, bar the windows and get an unlisted phone number. If necessary, hide—it may be better than being someone's easy target. The main thing is this: do whatever you must to create your own peace and safety; do *not* depend solely on police or court orders to solve your problem.

War is hell and that's no joke. You should do everything in your power to avoid it, but do *not* attempt the impossible and do *not* surrender your rights or your self-respect. If your spouse is in the picture, cares about the terms of the divorce, and disagrees about what the terms and arrangements should be, then you have only two possibilities: work it out or fight. Or you can fight for a while and then work it out, an unfortunately common pattern. Sooner or later, however, over 90% of all cases settle before trial.

The first step toward avoiding the emotional carnage and financial waste of a legal battle is for you *both* to realize certain fundamental facts:
  • Recognize how much you have to lose and how little to gain—no one really wins a legal battle for divorce.
  • Understand the destructive effect a bitter fight can have on you, on your kids and future co-parenting relations.
  • Understand that for the vast majority of issues, the outcomes in court are fairly predictable.
  • If you are opposed to the divorce but it seems to be happening anyway, try to understand and accept it. It is going to happen whether or not you accept it, and with more or less predictable terms. So don't give up anything you don't have to, but try not to obstruct a reasonable settlement or make outrageous demands as a way of blocking the divorce—it won't work and will just make things worse.
  • Make sure your spouse has a copy of this book, then maybe you can discuss some of the facts, issues, and alternatives. At least you will both be aware of what a divorce is about and the consequences of combat.

After you carefully consider the above points, here's what you have to do to avoid or minimize a battle:
  1. Prepare your case (Chapter 7). Get the facts and figures down, refine the issues.
  2. Get informed by reading this book. Find out how the laws apply to your case and what the range of likely outcomes might be *in your local courts*. You may want to see a local lawyer for this information, preferably a certified family law specialist or other attorney who does a lot of divorce work and who knows the local judges. Don't hesitate to get more than one opinion, especially if the first one seems to complicate your case. Anyone

can make a case complicated—you want simplification.

3. Learn the self-help tools for dealing with anger and reducing conflict (below).

4. Learn how to negotiate (below).

5. Consider the possibility of putting off a permanent settlement of terms until time goes by and emotions settle, trying instead to create temporary or short-term solutions. This strategy is only for people who can be expected to return to their normal, reasonable selves after the upset passes.

6. Try to negotiate for something within the range of likely outcomes. Don't ask too much; don't give up too much out of guilt, fear, or just to avoid a struggle. Try first to agree on the facts, then try to establish and expand on your areas of agreement. If all else fails, agree to disagree—agree to peacefully put the facts before a judge and let the judge decide.

7. Give serious thought to getting professional help from a counselor or mediator to assist you in working out an agreement. A good mediator can be very effective and a few hundred spent on mediation is better than thousands spent on legal conflict. Your goal is to get agreement, but a fall-back goal is to narrow the range of disagreement and limit the scope of battle. Mediation requires the cooperation of both spouses, although even without the participation of your spouse you can still get advice on how to handle your own end of things. You may want to try first to work things out yourself, but don't wait until you are both solidly entrenched in your respective positions. If there is a custody dispute that you can't settle, you are *required* to see a court mediator before you get to a court hearing.

If all efforts fail—if, for any reason, you and your spouse cannot reach an agreement—then you will end up in the Battle Group (Chapter 10) learning how to wage an efficient legal battle and how to minimize the damage to yourself and your children.

How to reduce conflict

Reducing conflict *never* means for you to compromise your rights or your self-respect, but it *is* hard work. Struggling with it can help *you* a great deal even if it doesn't actually reach your spouse or get you an agreement. Those are by-products. The real benefit is inside.

Conflict is what happens when two people have a different way of looking at the same facts or have to reconcile different goals and interests. It happens all the time; so what? *Healthy* conflict leads to solutions. It's not always easy, but you can usually work things out through discussion and compromise. *Unhealthy* conflict is when negative emotions pervert or displace an otherwise honest disagreement. The emotions that fuel unhealthy conflict are a combination of each spouse's own ancient attitudes, experiences, and habits coupled with all the patterns and distortions built up in the relationship. Untangling any part of this terrible can of worms will be a blessing for the rest of your life.

If you are like most couples—and not just divorcers—you have a predictable pattern of interaction that doesn't work. You have your own personal set of triggers that will set you off more or less the same way every time, over and over again. You have habit patterns for dealing with disagreement that do not serve you well or solve any problems. It may not be intentional, it may not even be conscious, but you know each other's buttons and you both push them automatically, without even thinking, especially when feeling angry, frightened or guilty.

Don't do that anymore.

Maybe it doesn't take much of a push on a button to get your bell to ring; maybe you are so upset that it rings almost by itself. Maybe your spouse is in a highly emotional condition too, acting like someone you wish you never knew, and you are taking it all very personally. Don't do that either.

Stop letting your mate's moods dominate your life. That's over. You don't need to do it any longer. That's what divorce is for—you are not divorcing just your spouse, you are also divorcing yourself from all those old patterns that didn't work and won't work. The divorce starts to work for you when you learn to untangle yourself from all those ugly dances you used to do. If you just stop (not easy to do), your mate may keep on, but will eventually have to notice that it's a solo performance. If not, too bad, but your ex-mate's problems aren't yours. *Your* problem is how *you* act, how *you* feel, and how to handle your own life.

You probably can't control your mate, nor should you try to, but you have a better chance if you concentrate on healing your own emotions and controlling your own actions. That's your whole focus now. We are talking about controlling *actions* here, not feelings. Don't try to control your feelings, they are real and valid. Observe your feelings, accept them, but express them some other way.

Stop. Breathe. Don't react.

Pay attention to what's going on for you. Are you angry? Hurt? Afraid? ....What? Be curious; investigate yourself and the scene.

Stop. Breathe. Don't react. Say that over and over quietly to yourself whenever things start to pop loose.

Curiosity is a great attitude and a great tool. Even while an event is in progress, you can be trying to figure out what the anger is all about. Anger is the flip-side of fear. When someone is afraid, the least little thing will set them off into a crisis of reactive anger. Fear is mostly unconscious and usually about not having enough— not enough security, power, respect, love or stability. Fear is about loss of face, not being in control, not having enough money, fear of change, fear of responsibility, things like that. What is your spouse afraid of? What are *you* afraid of?

To figure out what anger is about, you have to listen. Honest, open listening is the best thing you can do when someone is angry. You don't have to buy into their anger or agree with their point-of-view, just understand. If you are sincerely trying to hear what the angry person is saying and understand what's behind the anger— if you are not reacting to it, defending yourself from it, arguing, denying, dismissing or patronizing—then their anger will have nothing to feed on and will spend itself sooner. The angry person often has to save face by staying huffy and self-righteous, but your attitude will be noticed and will have a cumulative effect over time.

The most constructive thing you can do—and this is a difficult ideal—is to try to figure out the habitual interaction patterns that never did and still don't work for you and your mate. More particularly, you want to understand the part you play. Don't try to change anything, not at first; just observe when it's happening. Stop. Breathe. Even if you don't untangle the web, taking this attitude will be a big improvement. Whenever you catch it happening, just observe, don't respond. Notice how easily you fall into the old routine, how bad you feel after. Ooops, did it again. It's hard to stop, like asking a trout not to flash at splashing flies; like quitting an addiction cold turkey, only harder because you probably aren't always aware when you are doing it. Breaking ancient bad habits will greatly increase your future happiness. You may be able to do it by yourself, but some good professional help could be very useful at this point.

Working on your self is the most interesting of all possible paths. It may be the hardest—and most rewarding—thing you will ever do. This is when you develop your sense of personal responsibility. You are breaking your psychological dependency on your spouse, no longer depending on your mate for your own sense of well-being and worth; you will no longer let your feelings be determined by your mate's moods and actions. You and *only* you are responsible for your feelings and your actions. It isn't your fault when you are down, or anyone else's, but it *is* your responsibility to get up.

When times are hard, pay special attention to your body. Take care of it; relax it; be good to it. This is a healing time. Eat well, get healthy. Slow down, be quiet, hole-up, nest. Get massage, work on those knots. Take hot baths and/or cold showers, whatever works. Feeling bad isn't so bad if you don't feel bad about it. Just let it happen; it's proof you're alive and learning.

You know how sometimes it's easy for you to see what's *really* going on between two arguing people? Or how you can observe other people's patterns when they can't? What if someone could do that for you now? This is a good time to get some third person to listen, observe, give you feedback and advice. That's what professional family counselors are trained to do. Counseling and how to choose a counselor are discussed on pages 118 to 121.

Friends are wonderful moral support, but don't take advice from just anybody. Listen only to people who have wisdom and experience. Being a friend and caring about you doesn't make that person qualified to give good advice. If your friend is helping you get worked up, dwell on grievances or wallow in your stuff, get your advice somewhere else.

Practical Pointers:

1. Anger is not reasonable. When someone reaches the flash point, the ability to reason gets less as anger increases. Don't bother trying to talk sense until the anger is well past. Anger always passes. It runs its course faster if you don't feed it, faster yet if you use de-fusing techniques (below).

2. Deal with the problem, not the person.

3. You do not have to give in or be a doormat. **Rights:** You have the right to act in your own best interest; to respect and stand up for yourself; to express ideas and honest emotions; to ask for what you want; to set limits; to be treated with respect and dignity; to make mistakes and accept responsibility. **Responsibilities:** It is your responsibility to respect and honor the same rights for your mate; to take responsibility for your own behavior.

4. How to be assertive *and* constructive: **Confront** the problem, not the person. **De-fuse** the hostility, don't play at patterns that don't work. Your goal is to keep things calm so you can deal with the problem or complete the business at hand. **Disengage** from the conflict. Pay attention to your own anger level; when necessary, express your need to interrupt the cycle and allow a cooldown period. Re-schedule another time to work on the problem, then get up and quietly leave.

5. De-fusing: Here are some basic techniques for de-fusing anger when you run into it:
• First, remain calm yourself. Don't react. Instead, use your sense of curiosity; become an interested observer. Encourage talking by listening openly.
• *Show* that you understand or are trying to. Nod, paraphrase and mirror what you hear (Let's see if I have this right; you are saying that ......"). You must be sincere in this for it to work well.
• Talk to your spouse with "I" messages instead of the accusing "you." For example, "I can't discuss this when the TV is on so loud," instead of "You are noisy and totally inconsiderate."
• Make statements about yourself when necessary, but *not* about your mate personally. Be specific and concrete, be positive not negative.
• Set your limits ("If you keep yelling, I am going to leave," or "If you are more than 30 minutes late picking up the children, I will have to leave with them.").
• Don't defend or attack, don't generalize ("You always do this to me"), don't be sarcastic or discuss your mate's motives or dig up old history.
• Deal with the specific matter now at hand.
• Reassure your mate; help him or her to save face.
• Remember, your goal is to reach agreement, not score points.

6. Work with the attitude that you want to find solutions that allow you *both* to get what you want and need. Avoid the win/lose attitude.

112

7. Don't expect a quick-fix or miracles. You can do all the right things and not have immediate results. It's like erosion, the sort of thing you have to chip away at. It takes time, but you *will* succeed if you keep at it.

There is a wealth of popular material on dealing with anger and conflict; how to be assertive in a constructive way; and some very good material on how to talk and listen to your family. It can only help if you read some of it. Take a look at the reading list in the Appendix for some recommended titles.

Negotiating the terms of settlement

The most important predictor of a good divorce outcome is *client* rather than attorney control of the negotiation process. This doesn't mean you should not get help and advice from an attorney when you want it, it means you are better off if you plan to do most or all of the negotiating yourself. It is also realistic, because studies indicate that attorneys don't actually give much help or guidance anyway.

For example: In a 1976 Connecticut study, nearly half of those interviewed reported no more than three contacts with their attorney, *including* phone calls, while 60% reported that they had worked out all issues without attorney help. In a New Jersey Study in 1984, which considered only cases with children where *both* spouses had attorneys, less than 20% felt their lawyers had played a major role in settlement negotiations.

So, you see, chances are that you are going to end up dealing with the negotiation anyway, and there is strong evidence that you are far better off if you do. You get a higher degree of compliance with terms of agreement, a much lower chance for future courtroom conflict, and a lot more general good will. This is especially important if you have children and co-parenting to consider.

It obviously takes two to negotiate but, more than that, the parties must both *want* to negotiate. Ideally, you would each care about the other and want a solution that is comfortable or at least acceptable to you both. Lacking that, you may get through on a simple sense of frugality and self-preservation—seeking merely to avoid the extreme cost and unpleasantness of a battle. If your spouse doesn't want to negotiate, you may have to go ahead with the legal action first and hope for an improved attitude as the case moves on. Statistics show that about 90% of all spouses will *eventually* come to terms without a trial.

If your spouse won't negotiate, just start the divorce action anyway, on your terms. Make it very clear that you'd rather work things out together and are still willing to, but you are not willing to wait indefinitely. Doing the divorce paperwork yourself (Chapter 8) would be much less threatening to your spouse and less of an escalation: it shows that you, at least, are dealing with things personally, and it leaves your spouse the choice of dealing with things personally or going to a lawyer. You can always turn things over to a lawyer later.

Don't expect negotiating with a spouse to be easy; it isn't. There are lots of built-in difficulties—so many that you may want professional help from a good mediator. (See box, below, on the most common obstacles to negotiation.)

OBSTACLES TO NEGOTIATION

Here, adapted from an excellent academic study by Kenneth Kressel, *The Process of Divorce*, are notes on the most common obstacles you can face in a divorce negotiation:

High levels of emotion and conflict:

A certain amount of emotion, conflict and anger is normal in any divorce, but can easily become escalated into destructive conflict. In general, there are three sources of emotional upset:

• *Lack of mutuality* in the decision to divorce, a major difference in attitude about the need and desirability to end the marriage. This may be the single most important cause of conflict and hardest to deal with because it leaves one spouse consciously or *unconsciously* inclined to obstruct progress toward a final settlement.

• *Particular events*—for example, another lover, low finances, distressed children. This causes conflict due to jealousy over other relationships, fear of loneliness or financial hardship, guilt over leaving, and so on.

• *Separation distress*, normal to breaking psychological attachment, may be most intense just when you need to negotiate. A study showed that a high degree of difficulty at negotiation was felt by 33% of those with a high degree of attachment to their mates, only 3.3% of those with moderate attachment (ten times less!), and 25% of those with low attachment. The last figure may imply difficulty caused by an impaired ability to care for the needs of another. Where there is high attachment, it is obviously better to wait, if possible, to see if it can be reduced before negotiating.

Established negative patterns:

Spouses are often stuck in their bad habits. Unhappy spouses try to influence each other with criticism, insults, complaint and counter-complaint; they get locked into long chains of reciprocal negative behavior. Of all patterns of negative behavior, the least likely to work out well are situations where communication is shut down and spouses avoid any form of conflict, and where there is a very high level of *destructive* conflict, argument, and anxiety.

Okay, so there are problems—but what to do?

Get prepared, just like we've talked about throughout this book. Prepare your case and prepare yourself. Get control of the facts of your own divorce; understand how the law applies to the facts; find out the probable outcomes under the law; clarify your rights and your goals. To negotiate, you can also prepare by trying to understand your respective emotions and your past patterns. Just the fact that you are trying will help make things better.

It would be a very good idea for you to learn about negotiating. Reading a book on weight-lifting won't grow muscles and reading about negotiation won't make you a skilled negotiator, but it *will* make you better informed and more confident. There are many good books, but one of the easiest to read is the little (150 page) Penguin paperback by Fisher and Ury, *"Getting to Yes: Negotiating Agreement Without Giving In."* The chapter titles are a check-list for things you need to know:
- Don't bargain over positions
- Separate the people from the problem
- Focus on interests, not positions

High levels of stress:
Very few events in life generate as much stress as divorce. High stress impairs judgment, flexibility, tolerance, and creativity in problem solving. Stress reduces sensitivity to others, increases aggression. You may both be low on exactly the qualities you need at this time.

Inadequate resources:
Needing to support two households on the same old income puts a strain on your ability to negotiate. Fear of hardship leads to intransigence, inability to think creatively. When there's not enough to go around, there's nothing to use for trade-off. Personal psychology tends to get focused on or projected into feelings about money.

Inexperience at negotiation:
You or your spouse may not know the first thing about negotiating. One or both of you may be vague, unprepared, even ignorant of the basic facts of your own divorce, such as family income, debts, cash-flow, and so on. You may not know what you need or what you want; your goals may not be formulated. This,

fortunately, is something you can definitely do something about ....by working through this book.

Loss of face or self-esteem:
Making concessions can sometimes be felt as a weakness or a threat to self-esteem or public image, thus leading to stubbornness and belligerence. You may need to prove that you are a good parent or that you can come out ahead (or see that your mate doesn't) on the decision to divorce.

Different degrees of power and sensitivity:
Spouses generally have very different amounts of concern with winning, aggression, nurturing, sensitivity. Materially, one will tend to have more economic security and a stronger negotiating position. A professional mediator tries to equalize these differences.

- Invent options for mutual gain
- Insist on using objective criteria
- What if they are more powerful?
- What if they won't play?
- What if they use dirty tricks?

Meet only when you are emotionally calm and prepared. To help keep things neutral, safe and business-like, try to meet only at pre-arranged times and at comfortable, neutral places. Don't meet at your own home—it's too personal, someone may feel at a disadvantage, and you can't leave if you need to. You can deal with personal matters any time you wish, but do *not* talk business just any old time and place it happens to come up—you need to prepare, to compose yourself each time.

Start by making a list of the things you can agree on. Write them down. This is how you build a foundation for agreement and begin to clarify the major issue(s) between you. Next, write down the things you don't agree on, always trying to refine your differences—to make them more and more clear and precise. Try to break differences down into digestible, bite-sized pieces. This is very important: avoid taking a position until well after you have discussed the interests—needs, wants, fears, concerns—that you are both working with.

Show that you understand or are trying to understand your mate. State each other's view of things. Be very respectful of each other and each other's views. Watch body language carefully. Try to sense if there are unstated issues. Keep problems in the context of your shared common-ground. Keep in mind what will happen—the best and worst alternatives for each of you—if negotiations fail. Address facts and problems, not personalities. If you get stuck, refer to the legal standards of fairness and work within the range of predictable outcomes. Develop trust by being trustworthy; be open and share information.

Don't threaten or respond to threats; stick to the merits and your principles. Acknowledge the merits and principles stated by your mate. Especially do not attack your mate personally or threaten the negotiation itself. Don't try to buy a good relationship by giving concessions. Rewarding bad behavior will just get you more of the same; after all, it worked the last time.

It may take time to shift your mutual orientation from combative to competitive to co-operative. So don't just *do* something; *stand* there! Take your time, especially if you are handling things without professional help. You may want to work out temporary solutions for certain issues. A gradual approach takes pressure off and allows emotions to cool.

Good negotiating depends on your ability to handle your own emotions and deal with your spouse's emotions by developing attitudes and using practical techniques like those described under "How to reduce conflict," above. Make allowances for the emotional condition of yourself and your spouse.

Here's an age-old technique that really works to break some deadlock disagreements over property. Agree that one spouse will divide all the property into two piles in any way at all. Then the other spouse gets to choose which pile he or she will take. Flip a coin to see who divides and who chooses. This puts pressure on the spouse doing the dividing to make the piles so even that it won't matter which one gets picked.

If you have difficulty negotiating, it would be very reasonable for you to get help from a professional mediator. Good ones can often be effective very quickly. For example, each year, about 5,000 cases with custody disputes are referred for mandatory mediation to the Los Angeles County Family Court Services for compulsory mediation. Spending only a few hours per case, the county counselors manage to resolve over 60% of those custody disputes, and that's for the most hard-core 10% of all L.A. cases.

Every year, tens of thousands of couples settle their divorces by themselves with no help other than the practical legal information and the model marital agreement in *How To Do Your Own Divorce*. Chances are good that you can work things out yourself, but if you find the going rough and hard, don't keep struggling too long; don't wait until you are both at war from entrenched positions; don't get frustrated; don't get depressed; don't get mad—get help.

Mediation and counseling

There are times when a third person (just the right third person) can really help with some well–chosen words of advice, some feedback on how something looks from the outside, another point of view, a new idea for how to handle a situation. When you can't see the forest for the trees, you often get tangled up in tree roots—worse, you get lost. So maybe you should hire a guide.

There are two questions about involving a third person in your divorce. What can you get out of it and who do you get to do it? In broad terms, there are two kinds of professional help to consider—mediation and counseling. Either one can be extremely useful but the two activities are quite different.

The goal of counseling is mental health and emotional growth, usually of one individual client. A counselor can help you not only to understand and accept yourself, but also to make constructive changes in your habits and attitudes. Counseling can be quite practical and goal-oriented or it can be directed more toward therapy and personal transformation. From previous discussions, you have already been cued to situations where you could use help and support with the difficult job of digging into your own process and dealing with your life. That's what counseling is about.

To get help, you have to want it. You have to be ready, willing, and able to accept it. One person can get help from counseling, but to mediate, you *both* have to want to do it. You also have to be willing to make full disclosure of all facts and you have to trust that your spouse will not be lying or concealing facts. One of the few disadvantages of mediation as compared to court battle is that information cannot be taken under oath and there is no penalty for lying.

The goal of mediation is specifically to help a couple reach an agreement. As well, mediators will usually make the protection of children a goal (if not, they should). Another goal of mediation—one that many mediators overlook—is to help bring some order to your disagreements; to narrow and sharpen them so if a conflict can't be avoided, it can at least be limited to real issues. This makes any subsequent legal contest more efficient and less expensive.

The mediator is an objective, neutral person who has developed communication and counseling skills specifically targeted on con-

118

flict resolution and negotiation. The mediator works to equalize the bargaining power of the spouses; to bring all the facts out into the open; to get both spouses to develop and express their interests; to create and explore options; to seek creative alternatives; and to reach agreement. The mediator works for the couple, not one spouse or the other.

The mediator is usually either a licensed marriage counselor or a lawyer. There are no hard and fast rules, but a counselor may tend to be better at working with the emotional issues and communication difficulties that are the real cause of conflict. Lawyer-mediators will know more about the laws, likely outcomes of cases, and contractual aspects of settlement agreements. Lawyers will usually tend to be more business-like and emphasize negotiation.

Team mediation—a trend of growing popularity that we recommend strongly as being particularly effective—uses two mediators, a male and a female, one a lawyer and the other a counselor. That way all bases are covered and a richer, safer environment is created for problem solving.

Who can you go to for help?

You have to be careful who you take advice from, who you let guide you. What if you take bad advice and things don't go as well as they might—who pays the price? You do. Actions you do or do not take will have important consequences for the rest of your life. So will words you do or do not say, and choices you do or do not make. So who do you listen to?

A lot of people know a little bit and a few people know a lot. You can get advice from friends, relatives, or work-mates—often without even asking for it—but many people don't really know what they are talking about. Something might sound good because it feels comfortable or because you already agree with it or because it comes from someone you know and like, yet still be dead wrong—just plain bad advice.

The person you want to listen to, who can give you the most help, will be objective, neutral, trustworthy, wise and well–informed. They will be very good with people, know what they are doing, and have a lot of experience with a wide variety of divorce scenarios. Sounds like a professional job, doesn't it?

The very best way to find professional help is by personal reputation. It may be useful to know if the person you are considering has some license or certificate, but neither one is a reliable guarantee that the practitioner is good, or the right one for you. It would be ideal if you could get a recommendation from someone you know and trust who has used a certain professional with good results on a problem very much like yours. That's asking a lot, so let's assume you are just shopping around. Here are some things to consider:

- Try to get a recommendation from someone reliable. Ask around; talk to other professionals in related fields; call on local divorce support groups or family support agencies. If nothing else, look in the yellow pages under Divorce Assistance; Attorneys; or Marriage and Family Counselors.
- Unless you are certain about your choice, interview more than one prospective counselor or mediator.
- Ask about their fee schedule.
- Ask what percentage of their cases come to a successful conclusion.
- Ask about their training and background. Are they licensed? How long have they been in business? Do they do it full-time? Are they well-established locally?
- Ask about their specific area of expertise, how much experience they have had, and what other services they provide. You want someone who has a lot of experience with exactly the kind of work you want.
- Ask what their goals are and try to get a sense of the style and approach they use in cases like yours.
- Do they ask you questions, too, to find out if their service is the most appropriate? Do they explain what they do and do they distinguish mediation from counseling, or their type of counseling from other approaches?
- Do they ask what else you have tried to do to solve your problems?
- Does their work place feel calm and private?
- Do they discuss your options with you?

Finally, the most important thing to consider is not a rational process at all—the person you work with has to *feel* right to you. Mediation and counseling are intensely personal; both depend on the personal force of the professional. Whatever it is that works happens on the level of personalities—yours and theirs. So you need to find a professional with strength of character, depth, experience, wisdom—and a personality that suits you. Without these, not all the techniques, theories, and education in the world will really do the trick.

In mediation, the mediator has to be acceptable to both spouses. Mediation and counseling work through an interchange of personalities between the professional and the client. Far more than any amount of book-learning or study of techniques, it is the professional's personal strength of character and life-experience that makes mediation and counseling effective. So you have to use your instinct as the final vote after you have inquired about knowledge, training and experience.

When you reach an agreement

When you reach a final agreement, write it down immediately, right there on the spot, in the clearest, most specific language you can manage. Be thorough, detailed, and complete. If you both sign it, it will be binding unless you goofed in some way. *(Option: start it with, "We intend to agree as follows....," then you both sign it and each keep a copy. This is not a binding contract yet because of the word "intend," but rather it is a solemn ceremony and reminder of all the points and details you agreed to.)* Still moving purposefully and letting no grass grow under your feet, draw it up formally as a contract—use the model agreement in *How To Do Your Own Divorce*—and get it signed and notarized right away. Now it is definitely binding. If a lot is involved, one or both of you may want to see a lawyer—perhaps the same lawyer at the same time—before you sign. This is to make sure you understand the fine points and haven't left out anything important or inadvertently used troublesome wording. In fact, you may want a lawyer to draw the agreement in the first palce. Let the lawyer improve your agreement, but don't let anyone confuse you or talk you out of your agreement without getting a second opinion and thinking it over.

Once your agreement is in hand, go back to Chapter 8 and read about how to handle an agreed divorce. The hard part is over, the rest is just detail work and red-tape.

What if you can't agree?

After all our talk about the advantages of reaching agreement, it is finally time to face the fact that you can't always get one no matter what you do. Or maybe working with your spouse on an agreement is not something you want to do under any circumstances. Maybe you just want what you are entitled to and that's all.

It all amounts to the same thing. If you can't settle you have to battle. If you have to battle, you may as well learn how to do it in the most efficient and cost-effective way possible—and while you're at it, learn how to minimize the damage. So move on to Chapter 10 and join the Battle Group.

10

How To Win a
Controlled Legal Battle

If you have to fight, you might as well learn how to do it efficiently, so welcome to the Battle Group. Notice that the chapter title says "legal" battle—you do not *need* to battle on a personal or emotional level in order to win a legal battle. Notice that the title says "controlled" battle—people hardly ever win an *un*controlled battle. This chapter is where you learn how to control a legal battle when you can't (or don't want to) avoid one, how to battle efficiently and effectively, and how to minimize the damage.

Damage control

Have you already read above about how expensive a legal battle is and how emotionally destructive it can be? It is all true. You should never get into a legal battle if you can possibly avoid it. On the other hand, you should not surrender your rights or your self respect in order to avoid a fight. If you end up in a battle, it is essential that you understand what you are getting into, then do everything possible to minimize the damage and protect yourself and your children.

Commercial airlines are required by law to tell passengers that parents must always put on their own oxygen mask first, then take care of their children. You can't help a child if you pass out in the process. Same with divorce; you have to be okay before you can help anyone else. So, the first thing you do to protect your kids from harm in a divorce battle is to protect yourself—to develop and maintain your own sense of well-being.

Protecting yourself
The issues in a divorce conflict are almost always emotional ones that get played out in terms of property, money and children. As a

tool of emotional warfare, the legal battle is the ultimate button a spouse can push; the same kind of decision that can launch armies or the ultimate missiles. *You are inviting terrible harm to yourself to whatever extent your legal battle is an extension of the emotional conflict you have been conducting with your mate all along.*

The most effective technique is for you to *keep business and emotions separate.* As far as you should be concerned, a divorce battle is strictly a matter of business. It should be run strictly according to reason and practical considerations. If your spouse gets confused and trapped into an emotional conflict, don't react; don't get involved in it at that level. If your spouse or your spouse's attorney use tactics that are upsetting, don't give them the satisfaction of letting it work on that level. Go back and take a look at the suggestions in Chapter 4 for keeping the divorce on a business level.

To survive a legal battle with minimum damage, you *must* free yourself *unilaterally* from the old patterns that you and your mate were trapped in. Never mind what your spouse does or says—that's not your concern now; your job is to get out of it from *your* end. That means dismantling a part of your own internal process. Psychological traps like self-blame or blaming your spouse (see Chapter 3) are like cement blocks on your legs—they will drag you down for sure. You have to free yourself from the old emotional battle and conduct your legal battle as a piece of business.

The check-list for what you have to do to minimize emotional damage to yourself is like an incantation or a prayer that can protect you. Repeat this over and over to yourself as you prepare for battle:

> "I will do what's right, I will do what I must, I will do what I can, and I will do my best, but I will *not* worry about the rest—it is out of my hands and my well-being does not depend on it."

Do what's right: To get through a battle relatively unscathed, you will need the strength that comes from a clear conscience and moral certainty.

• You must be certain that you want only what is rightfully yours and what is best for the children. Is what you want within the range of probable outcomes—is it *clearly* supported by the facts and the rules of law? Be *sure* to get more than one lawyer's opinion before you fight.

• You must be very clear that you are not acting out of anger, guilt, fear or greed—that you are not seeking revenge, not trying to punish or control your spouse. You must be certain that you are not merely continuing the old emotional conflict.

You will be protected from emotional damage by the strength that comes from knowng in your heart that what you are doing is right and unavoidable—that you have made every effort to be flexible. Without this, the legal battle can turn your life into pure hell.

Do what you must: You must know that you have done everything in your power to avoid this battle. It should be perfectly clear that in order to protect your rights, you have exhausted all other alternatives and have no better choice than to go to the lawyers and courts. On the other hand, you should never just roll-over and give in just to have it done with. You should never feel guilty for insisting on your rights or for refusing to sacrifice your self-respect.

Do what you can: We all live within the limitations of what is possible. There is no blame for failing to achieve any goal, only for failing to make the effort and to use whatever talents and resources that are available to you. If you have a right or a child to protect or some dignity to preserve and you fail to make the effort, then you have not done what you can.

Do your best: You can't control others, you can't control most events, you can only do your best. Like everyone else out there, you are an imperfect and fallible human being, so there's no sense in punishing yourself if you occasionally fall short of perfection. If things don't go your way, you don't have to blame yourself if you know that you gave it your best effort. Instead, give yourself a reward and take some credit for your good intentions and for having tried so hard.

Don't worry about the rest: If you do what's right, what you must, what you can, and give it your best, you will discharge all personal obligations in the matter. This is like the ancient practice of writing troubles and prayers on paper that you then cast into a river. You have committed your case into the unfathomable processes of the legal system, so the matter is out of your hands and the outcome is no longer in your control. There's no point in worrying about it or being attached to it.

Whenever you get caught up in conflict or feel ground down by it, repeat this a few times: "I have done what's right, I did what I had to, I did what I could, and I have done my best, so I will *not* worry about the rest—it's out of my hands and I don't depend on it."

It is very important to adopt an attitude and a life-style that does not depend on the outcome of the battle or on anything your spouse says or does. This doesn't mean you shouldn't care about it or try your best, but don't let your well-being depend on the outcome. While the legal battle drags on—and it may be quite a long time—you should explore other avenues and build a foundation out of the other resources in your life. The legal wheel is turning and the chips may or may not come to you when it stops. Meanwhile, get on with building your life.

Protecting your children

Go back and read page 36, "Rules of the Road #2—Getting Your Children Through a Tough Time."

Studies show that harm to children is more closely related to conflict *after* the divorce. Everyone has conflict before and during a divorce, but if you want to protect your children, get finished with the conflict and resolve it, at least within yourself, as quickly as possible.

Children need their relationship with both parents. There is a bonding that cannot easily be replaced by a surrogate parent or step-parent. To protect the essential parent-child relationship, you have to insulate children from your own conflict with their other parent. The divorce is not their problem; it's yours. Being a bad wife or husband does not make your spouse a bad parent. So, don't hold the children hostage—they are not pawns or bartering pieces in your game. In the area of custody and visitation, don't bargain with your spouse on any other basis than what will give your children the most stability and the best contact with both parents.

The worst thing for the child of a broken home is feeling responsible for the break-up and feeling that loving one parent is a betrayal of the other. These feelings cause children intense stress and insecurity. To protect your child from almost unbearable pain, don't say anything bad about the other parent in front of the child; don't undermine or interfere in any way with the child's relationship with or love for the other parent; don't put the child in a

126

position of having to take sides. Do encourage every possible kind of constructive relationship your child can have with your ex-mate. Let the children know that you are happy when they have a good, loving time with their other parent.

Kids can really get on your nerves at a time like this and single parenting is enough to overwhelm any normal person. You are not Superman or Mary Marvel and kids are not designed to be raised by one lone person. You need help and support, and you need time off from the kids. Make a point of getting help from family, friends and the many parent support groups and family service agencies throughout California. Get references to groups in your area through local churches, through your County Conciliation Court, or by calling 1-800-222-5465.

Winning strategies—hardball or softball?

What does "winning" mean to you? Think about it. You have certain goals to pursue and rights to protect—that's all. The first and most important thing you do to "win" is to immediately stop thinking about winning and your spouse losing. Divorce isn't that kind of contest and a relationship is not a battlefield. If you think that way, you are setting yourself up to be a loser. Separate yourself from the contest emotionally and conduct this strictly as a piece of business.

Never start a divorce contest on the strength of a single opinion. Take your case around for a variety of advice. This is essential: don't skimp at this critical step in your case. Ask your lawyer: are your demands reasonable under the law? Ask yourself: are your goals worth the price of the battle?

What *are* your goals for this legal contest? Whatever your other goals, there is one that should always have top priority—to *negotiate* an acceptable settlement. Everything you and your attorney do should be aimed at getting your spouse and your spouse's attorney into good-faith negotiations that will lead to an agreement that you can both accept. Okay, what strategy do you use to do that?

There are two basic types of divorce strategy, defensive and aggressive. Which should you use? Well, when anxious hikers asked what to do if they ran into a bear, the old woodsman

explained it to them. One school of thought, he said, holds that you must stand perfectly still until the bear goes away, but other experts say you're better-off banging pots, screaming and waving your arms. Studies show that both schools are right about half the time ...it all depends on the bear. In divorce, everything depends on you and your spouse until the lawyers come in, then it depends on four personalities. If you add some therapists, we have a whole party of variables. It gets hard to work out or second-guess what is best—something that only gets clear after it's all over.

Hardball or softball? Softball is a civilized, easy-going approach to the legal contest. Your purpose is only to stick to what you think is right and, if necessary, let some judge decide. It is a decision to disagree peacefully, to let the lawyers do their job and the legal process take its course. If you can't agree, why get upset? Let the judge decide. Hardball, on the other hand, is a tough, aggressive strategy. If your spouse is being bad or is likely to cheat, you have to defend your rights very forcefully—and you might have to show some teeth. If your spouse is the one who starts being legally aggressive, you have a choice—respond in kind or be defensive.

Aggressive cases are those in which you are on the offensive. You move fast; you hire an aggressive lawyer to take the legal field and strike hard. You fire off a full range of legal motions and go to hearings to freeze accounts, put your spouse under court orders to behave, and set rigid visitation schedules for children. You send out volumes of legal interrogatories (questions) and demand boxes of documents and paperwork. Aggression costs a great deal of money and can destroy future hopes for good personal and co-parenting relationships. It can damage your children, maybe permanently. But, in some cases, it might be necessary.

One goal might be to get what you have been denied: honest information, your fair share of the community property, access to your children, relief from abuse, and the like. Another goal may be to make a dramatic statement to your mate—a cold splash of legal realism as shock therapy. You are showing teeth in the hopes that it will lead to negotiation. However, aggression is risky business that can back-fire. It depends on the temperament of your spouse *and* your spouse's attorney. Avoid the trap of using legal aggression to punish or harass your spouse—that sword cuts two ways and you *will* get hurt. It isn't worth it. You should use aggression only if forced into it by circumstances beyond your control.

To conduct an aggressive case, you will be looking for an aggressive lawyer who is also experienced, bright, tough, and tenacious. Spend some time interviewing various lawyers about their philosophies and attitudes. If, for example, a lawyer is *eager* to attack, that lawyer may be just as quick to attack you if a difference of opinion arises. Look for someone who goes to battle reluctantly, who is always looking for a way to cool the battle down, but who can punch it out if necessary. Read more about choosing your lawyer in Chapter 11.

Defensive cases are those where your spouse is on the attack and is coming on hard and strong. Don't get mad; this is business. Your choice here is either to conduct a stubborn defense or to go on the offensive. If you do the least possible to protect your position, you conserve your energy and money while waiting for your mate's team to run out of steam. A quiet defense may make it easier to negotiate an agreement later. A good defense is almost always more comfortable and less expensive. Let them do the work; let them bark and growl; you can just rely on the facts and the legal process.

If your mate's attorney is unusually aggressive or if they play dirty tricks, like making the case unnecessarily expensive with a flood of paperwork and motions in court, you may decide to play their game. If you counter-attack and drag your mate personally through some depositions and hearings, maybe you'll convince your mate to negotiate. But first, ask some questions or yourself and of your attorney:

- Have they got the facts right?
- Does the law support their position?
- Are they aiming anywhere near the probable outcome?
- Is your mate's position or personality vulnerable somewhere?
- Is this going to be worth the expense?
- What's the advantage of striking back compared to just letting it go to court? What do you have to gain? What can you lose?

The strategy you decide to use always depends on knowing very clearly what your goals are, then you consider the facts and circumstances, and the personalities of the people—you, your spouse, your attorneys. Then you make your decisions and choices.

Obviously, softball is the better game. It costs less and hurts less. If you don't have to worry about bad or dishonest behavior, let the lawyers negotiate and the judge decide what can't be agreed.

Even if you get into an aggressive battle, you should always be looking for ways to cool it down and to negotiate an agreement.

How to fight effectively at less expense

1—Know exactly what you want from the battle
The most important part of preparation for battle is thought. Don't go to war without it. Think about your case, your life, and get very detailed and specific about what you want: property, support, future relationships for yourself and your children, life goals and values. Sometimes all you want at first is more information that your spouse won't give you, or a check on what has been given. Your lawyer can get information under oath. At some point, you will have all the information there is, then you will have to decide finally what you ultimately want.

Planning your battle strategy—even to the type of attorney you choose—depends on a clear understanding of what you want to accomplish in the battle. What property do you want? How much support? How much do you care about future relations between you and your spouse or the emotional well-being of your children and their relationship with their other parent?

2—Try to narrow the issues
Before you get into a battle and all during the fight, do whatever you can to narrow the issues. This means you try to agree with your spouse, in writing, to as many points as possible. Sometimes you can agree to a whole lot of things, then agree that you disagree on certain remaining issues and that you will let the court decide. A battle is much more efficient when conducted on a narrow front. Be very cautious about taking advice to broaden the battle! It may indeed strengthen your bargaining position if you ask far more than you want or attack an issue you don't care about, but it can also stimulate the opposition, undermine your credibility, and prolong the battle.

3—Set the tone of the battle
If you care at all about keeping the level of conflict as low as possible, then be sure to keep your spouse informed at all times and well ahead of time about what you and your lawyer are doing and why you are doing it. This helps to minimize unpleasant surprises,

130

misunderstandings and over-reaction, especially if your spouse returns the favor. It helps to keep the background lines of communications open. Communicate by letter to avoid arguments; keep copies. Remember, most cases eventually get settled by the spouses between themselves, not by their lawyers, so you will be better off for trying to keep communication lines open.

4—Carefully choose the right lawyer

It may be okay to rely on the first attorney you interview for information, but that's not good enough for a battle. It is *very* important to take your case around to several lawyers to get a variety of opinions and attitudes before you choose the one you want. Don't economize at the wrong time; paying for these extra interviews can save you a fortune later. Read Chapter 11, think about your objectives, then decide what lawyer you are going to work with.

5—Be thoroughly prepared and informed

When you go to see a lawyer, you don't want to waste any time—it costs too much. You should know your goals, be familiar with all facts of your case, and know as specifically as possible what you want to talk about with the attorney. Send the attorney a note before you go in, detailing exactly what you want to discuss, and include copies of any relevant documents. That gives the lawyer time to absorb your information and gives you a chance to see if the lawyer bothers to prepare for the conference.

Organize your papers and your thoughts; make an agenda before you go in. Keep notes on every discussion; keep track of time spent on the phone or in the office so you can compare it to the itemized billing.

6—Make it clear that you are in charge of your case

This is your life and you have to live with any consequences of the divorce action, so it is reasonable—and important—that you be ultimately in charge of your own case. You want to hire the lawyer's knowledge and experience; you very much want to listen to the lawyer's good advice; but you expect to be part of any decisions that affect the tone and strategy of the case. You will be ultimately responsible.

Tell the lawyer that you would like copies of all papers and correspondence, and that you expect to be kept informed of every step in the action. Also make it clear that you expect your phone calls to be returned as soon as possible, no later than the next working day. In return, you have to reassure the lawyer that you will not be one of those clients that makes frivolous calls.

7—Don't hesitate to switch attorneys
If your attorney's services turn out to be unsatisfactory, you should send a letter with specific details of what the problem is and what changes you want made. If there is no improvement, start looking for another attorney. See Chapter 11 on firing an attorney.

11

How To Choose
and Use a Lawyer

Shopping for an attorney is exactly like shopping for melons. You should check the prices and make sure the one you choose "feels" right to you. You have a right to ask questions, look things over and be choosy about whom you hire to take on such a major personal role in your life.

Don't be intimidated. Call around on the telephone to find out how much it will cost just to meet the lawyer and see if you want to hire him. Ask what the hourly rates are (and if there is a flat fee if you have an uncontested case). If all you want is help with some specific part of doing your own dissolution (say, a marital settlement agreement) ask if they will do this and at what rate. Most attorneys will do the initial interview for a fairly small fee; rates thereafter run from $80 to $500 per hour, but $150 to $250 is quite common.

Before you see the attorney, be sure you are thoroughly prepared with the facts of your case and know exactly what you want to talk about. Have copies of all relevant documents and information ready. You might consider mailing the information in ahead of time so the attorney will have a chance to be prepared, too. Few attorneys will spend much time preparing for an initial interview, especially if they charge little or nothing for it. However, it can do no harm and it will show that you are business-like and thorough.

You want two things in your divorce attorney: expertise in divorces and a good attitude. A third thing is personal and hard to pin down, but your attorney must be someone you can trust and work with comfortably, someone that has your confidence. If the lawyer will be handling your whole case, it is hard to say which quality is most important—you need it all. However, if you just want information and advice or a contract drawn, the lawyer's attitude is less important than knowledge and experience because you are running your own case.

The best way to find a good divorce lawyer is on the recommendation of another professional (say, a divorce counselor) who has reason to know about divorce attorneys and their reputations. The next best way is on the personal recommendation of someone you know well and trust who has had a divorce and been pleased with a particular lawyer's services. Finally, your local bar association will have a referral service; look them up in the yellow pages and ask for a "certified family law specialist." Be very cautious with recommendations from people you do not know or where the service was not a divorce. It is not useful to know that a certain attorney is good at business, personal injury, or criminal work when what you want is a divorce.

In California, the State Bar certifies family law specialists. The specialist has taken the trouble to get extra professional training, sit for qualifying exams, and has shown a special interest in family law practice. Of course, many general practitioners are also excellent and well–qualified in the divorce arena. All things being equal, it would be better to have a family law specialist, so start shopping in that category. But all things are *not* equal. Knowledge, experience and expertise are very important, but attitude sits right at the top of any list and you can't get a certificate for it.

It is extremely difficult to judge a lawyer's technical competence, so for that you will have to rely on the the State Bar's specialist certification program, personal references and reputation. When shopping for attitude, it helps to know that there are several distinct types of divorce lawyers, distinguished by their attitudes on three key subjects: attitude toward the client, attitude toward therapists and counselors, and goals of legal activity. Below is a list based on lawyer types suggested in Ken Kressel's scholarly book, The *Process of Divorce*.

A field guide to divorce lawyer types

Here are three innocent questions that you should sprinkle through your first interview. Ask the attorney:
* What are your goals in this kind of case; what will you try to accomplish?
* What do you think is a good outcome for a divorce case?
* How do you feel about working with counselors, mediators, and therapists?

134

The way the attorney responds will reveal a lot about his or her attitude and will help you locate the attorney in the guide below. This is not fool-proof (especially if they have read this book) since lawyers are professional at showing the face they want you to see. Ultimately, you will be relying on your instincts.

1. The Cynic

This lawyer does not respect his client (or very many people, for that matter). Thinks his or her job is thankless and messy, and that the clients are emotionally unbalanced. Cynical about human nature generally, pessimistic that a good or constructive outcome is ever possible in divorce. Sometimes derogatory toward clients, especially behind their backs. Skeptical about the value of counseling; may refer clients to counseling, but mostly to get rid of the burden. Committed to helping a client "win" whatever they want. Dislikes disruption of schedules due to counselor's advice to wait. This one is hard to spot—rarely lets it show.

2. The Gallant Gladiator

Also known as a "hired gun," "mechanic," or "technician." Pragmatic and technical. Assumes clients are capable of knowing what they want. Thinks the lawyer's job is to evaluate the feasibility of the clients goals, then go for it. Unlike the Cynic, does not disparage clients. Thinks a good outcome is possible —"good" meaning to produce results for the client. Views counselors according to usefulness for evidence, as expert witnesses.

3. The Tiger/ Pugilist

An extreme variant of the cynic (the pugilist) or the gladiator (the tiger). Mauls the other side with a continuous barrage of motions, demands and legal maneuvers. Might intentionally be offensive to opposing attorneys; seeks to upset and wear down the opposition, to grind them into submission. Tiger thrives on the hunt, pugilist is just a thug. Dangerous to associate with as they may bite the hand that used to feed them.

4. The Mediator

Oriented toward compromise, negotiation, and rational problem solving. Emphasizes cooperation with the other side, particularly the other attorney. Appeals to client's better nature and assumes client wants "what's fair." Posture of emotional neutrality. Unlike the above types, tends to downplay (but not deny) the adversarial nature of lawyer's role. Fights only when provoked by the other side. May refuse to carry out aggressive, conflict oriented demands of client. A good outcome is one both parties can live with. Uses counselors to de-escalate conflict.

5. The Social Worker

Concerned for client's over all well-being, post-divorce adjustment, and (especially for females) employability. Keeps entire family in mind and concerned about long-range plans for children (camps, education, etc.) Sees that divorce is not usually an easy solution to marital unhappiness, but without the pessimism or rancor of the Cynic. Unlike above types, sees reconciliation as a professional obligation, not a waste of time. Has some enthusiasm for therapy, welcomes counselors in any stage of proceedings. Good outcome is one where client achieves social reintegration. Believes that social services and institutions for divorced families need to be expanded.

6. The Therapist

Accepts that client is in a state of emotional stress and turmoil. Assumes legal aspects can be adequately dealt with only by engaging the emotional ones; tries to understand client's motivation. Gets involved with reconciliation. Sees a good outcome as reintegration of client. Welcomes involvement of counselors. Thinks legal system not adequate for people's needs in divorce. Committed to reducing conflict wherever possible. Opposes belligerent, vengeful demands of client. Aware of tunnel–vision from getting only one side of the conflict, but still subject to it; frustrated by professional ethics prohibiting contact with the other spouse; tries round-about means to get insight into the other side.

7. The Moralist

Rejects neutrality, does not hesitate to use own sense of right and wrong. Gets involved. Will oppose client's demands when felt to be "right" and necessary. May aggressively address client's stance and try to "correct" client's attitude. Really strong about children; may demand client send child to counselor. Whether the Moralist's view is based on sound understanding of people or psychology is open to question. Good outcome is what satisfies the lawyer's sense of fair play, parental duties, right and wrong.

Questions to ask a lawyer

In addition to the questions suggested above about the lawyer's attitude and goals, you will want to ask:

About the attorney's background—
- how long have you been in practice?
- how long with this firm?
- what areas of law do you specialize in?
- what percentage of your practice is divorce?
- what percentage of your divorce cases are litigated?
    (lets you know how many settle without litigation)

About fees—
- how much do you charge? If you want a specific service, there may be a flat fee—so much, say, for a marital settlement agreement. Otherwise, it is likely to be an hourly rate. Either way, get it clear.
- how am I billed for your secretary's time or research by other staff?
- what costs can we anticipate?
- how much do you need to get started?
- is the initial retainer to be applied against future billings?
- if the retainer exceeds the billings, will the balance be returned?
- can I count on you to get your fee from my spouse, or am I going to be responsible for your payment and collection from my spouse?
- do you bill exactly for time spent, say for short phone calls, or do you round-off to a higher time period?

About other things—
- can I expect a copy of all papers and documents?
- do you need any information that you don't have yet?
- based on my facts, do you see any problems in this case?

Who to pick?

If you are only looking for advice on a particular subject, an appraisal of likely outcomes in your local courts, or help with drafting a marital settlement agreement, you are mostly concerned with the attorney's knowledge and experience. Attitude is less relevant here, as you are handling your own case. The only thing to watch out for is an attorney who seems to make things more confused rather than less, or who urges you to do things that could lead to conflict.

If you want an attorney to handle your divorce for you, the person you choose has a lot to do with your strategy and the current temperature of relations with your spouse. We suggest that you generally avoid anyone who seems cynical, unnecessarily aggressive, or moralistic. For most cases, you will want to look for someone who prefers to avoid conflict in favor of negotiation and compromise. You are trying to find an attorney who understands softball and prefers to keep the case cool. At the same time, you want someone who can slug it out if the other side gets aggressive.

Hardball: If your spouse plays dirty or is being very aggressive, you will want a formidable and aggressive attorney with lots of experience to protect you and slug it out. If you want an especially aggressive attorney, perhaps even a pugilist, be very cautious: you may end up with a tiger by the tail. An acquisitive, mercenary attorney can turn on you as easily as on your spouse.

Avoid situations where you don't like the way the attorney or the staff treat you. Avoid lawyers with a pushy, domineering personality; they may not listen to you or be willing to do things your way. Make sure the attorney knows it is your life and your case; that you are in charge.

Fees and retainer agreements

Divorce actions are always unpredictable, so lawyers rarely quote a flat fee for doing a divorce, but usually charge an hourly rate instead. Call around to see what the going rates are in your area. If, however, you are requesting a specific service, like writing a marital settlement agreement when the terms are all settled, then a flat fee is just what you want. Flat fees have the advantage of being more definite; you know exactly what the service will cost.

The law requires a *written* retainer agreement in any case that is likely to run over $1,000. The agreement must specify what work is to be done and the fee to be charged or the manner in which the fee will be calculated.

138

If you have little or no income or other assets, and your spouse has plenty of stable income, savings or other assets, then you should be looking for an attorney who will agree to take your case for out-of-pocket costs and collect all attorney's fees from your spouse. You want the retainer agreement to state clearly that the attorney will *only* seek compensation from your spouse and not from you under any circumstance. Many attorneys will work on this basis, but many won't, so you will have to shop around until you find someone with a good attitude.

Never agree to put up security for your attorney's fees. Do *not* sign a mortgage or trust deed on your home or any other property. If this is what the attorney wants, look around for another attorney.

Be very cautious of any attorney who asks for a fee that is contingent on the size of your recovery. That practice is generally inappropriate in divorce cases.

A retainer contract is something you negotiate like any other deal and there is no law that says it has to be a take-it-or-leave-it proposition. Attorneys with that attitude may be arrogant, stubborn and hard to work with on other levels, so keep looking. There are many ways that billing practices can work to your disadvantage, so you will want to examine and give careful thought to the details of any retainer agreement you are asked to sign. Take it home, study it, make sure you understand everything in it before you sign. Pay special attention to things it does not say. Discuss terms you don't understand and terms that you want removed, changed or added. It is okay to request and discuss terms that you would like but don't expect to get. That is the nature of negotiation.

Here is a list of terms to think about and negotiate over, more or less in order of importance to you:

• Be very clear that you do not pay for time spent negotiating the attorney's contract. The attorney is working for himself during that time, so billing should start only after the contract is signed.
• Make sure the retainer paid will be applied to future billings and not kept as a base fee for taking the case. Specify that any unused portions will be returned.
• Define time units billed and how fractions of hours are rounded off; avoid the common practice where you can get billed a quarter hour for a five–minute phone call.

• Request (insist on?) a detailed itemization on each billing that shows the date and time for each task, total time spent, and amount billed.

• Request a monthly billing.

• Inquire about charges, if any, for secretary and staff time. Request that amounts for time billed to secretaries, research assistants, paralegals or associate attorneys be billed separately. This is so you can see exactly what is going on and who is doing it.

• You may want it stated that you will not be responsible for associate attorneys or experts retained without your written consent.

• If your case is not terribly complex, ask that the contract specify that you will not be billed for research time. The high hourly rate implies that the attorney already knows his business.

• Try to get an agreement that you will not be billed for court time spent on continuances that you do not request or for any court time not actually in trial. You really don't want to pay $150 an hour for time spent just sitting around waiting to continue your case to some other day.

Here's a novel idea: consider offering an incentive fee where the attorney gets paid at a higher rate if your case is settled very quickly, in less than some specified number of hours. This rewards the attorney for fast, effective work. Conversely, the rate would go down if your case goes over so many hours or if it goes to trial. This is not a common practice but it may suit your case. It's just one more thing you can negotiate when getting into a retainer agreement.

How to use your lawyer

Using a lawyer efficiently. The most important thing is to be very well prepared whenever you contact a lawyer. Know your facts, know what you want to ask about, and know exactly what you want the lawyer to explain or do for you. Plan each conversation; make an agenda; write down the things you want to talk about; take notes on the content of every conversation; keep track of time spent on all phone calls and meetings. Keep a file for all your notes and all letters and documents. Do as much as possible on the phone and by mail to keep office time at a minimum.

Regard your attorney as a resource, not someone you cling to or depend on for emotional support and stability. A lawyer is not the right person to make your decisions or lead your life—you are. Lawyers cost too much for you to use them for sympathy and consolation—that's what family, friends and counselors are for.

When you talk to a lawyer, stick to the facts and don't just chat, ramble, or complain about things your spouse did unless you actually want your lawyer to do something about it. Don't take your anger to an attorney; you want your best interests represented, not your emotions.

Taking control of your own case. Being in control of your own case and your own life is the single best thing you can do in any divorce, so it is essential that you have a lawyer who can work cheerfully on that basis. If you are well prepared and business like, that will help the lawyer to see that you are in charge of things, but you should actually *say* that's how you want it to be. Tell the lawyer that you want good advice and will rely on the lawyer's experience, but that you expect to make decisions that concern the tone and strategy of the case. Ask that you be sent copies of all documents and letters. Let the attorney know that you expect phone calls to be answered by the next working day. These little things let the lawyer know you are the boss. After all, you pay the bills.

Using a lawyer for specific tasks. Instead of hiring a lawyer to get you a divorce, it may be far more cost-effective to use the lawyer just for information or advice on specific subjects. That may be all the legal help you will need. If not, you can always go back for more help later. After you have organized all your facts and read about how the law works in your case, if you still have questions about the law or what the likely outcome will be in your county, write all your questions down and ask a lawyer.

You may decide to have a lawyer help with your marital settlement agreement, either to draft one or just to check over one you have made yourself. If you get stuck or confused at any point in your divorce, that's a good time to go for help. The more specific and prepared you can be, the more you will get for your money.

How to fire your lawyer

If your lawyer is not performing to your satisfaction, you should send a letter (keep copies) setting out very specifically what needs to be changed. If there is no improvement, start shopping for another lawyer. Some things can't be changed: if you lose trust and confidence in your lawyer, you might want to start looking around for a replacement. Nothing is worse than to feel trapped in a bad relationship with your own attorney.

You have an absolute right to fire your attorney at any time for any reason or no reason at all, *whether or not any money is owed.* If you hire another attorney, the new one will take care of the transfer. Of course, you still owe your former lawyer for time spent.

You can also fire your attorney and take over yourself. You should definitely do this in writing *and keep a copy of the letter*. If documents have been filed on your behalf in a court, you must also send along a substitution of attorneys form, naming yourself as the new attorney "In Pro Per" (jargon that means you will be representing yourself). There is a form for substitution of attorneys at the end of this chapter that you can use as a guide for typing your own. Request the fired attorney's signature on the form, then file it with the court once it is signed. Your letter should demand that all files and papers be immediately forwarded to you. If the attorney delays or refuses to sign, go ahead and file it with just your signature alone. That should work, although having the attorney's signature would be better.

An attorney cannot legally or ethically delay signing the substitution of attorneys or balk at turning over files and documents merely to inconvenience you or to pressure you into payment of fees owing. Failure to promptly sign a substitution of attorneys or to forward files to you would constitute a breach of the attorney's duty. In case of unreasonable delay, fire off a letter of complaint to the local and State Bar associations with copies to your old attorney.

SUBSTITUTION OF ATTORNEYS

Your name
Your street address
City, State, Zip
Your phone number

Attorney for (Petitioner/ Respondent) In Pro Per

SUPERIOR COURT OF THE STATE OF CALIFORNIA

COUNTY OF . . . .

Marriage of   )
)   CASE NO.:   . . . .
. . . .)
          Petitioner,   )
)   SUBSTITUTION
)   OF ATTORNEYS
. . . .)
          Respondent,   )
)
_____)

        I, (Petitioner/ Respondent), hereby substitute myself,
(your name, address, telephone number) as my attorney of record in
this action, in lieu and in place of(name of your former lawyer).

Dated: . . . ., 19...   _____your signature_____
                                       (type your name)

I consent to the above substitution.

Dated: . . . ., 19...   _____
                                       (type name of former attorney)

APPENDIX

Recommended Reading

There are a lot of very good books out there, but to save you the trouble of wading through shelves of titles, we asked some leading counselors which books they regarded as classics. Asterisks indicate the author's pick. This isn't the definitive list, just a place to start, so keep looking, keep reading, keep learning. Ask people you know what helped them. That's the best way.

For Everyone:
Crazy Times, Abigail Trafford. Harper & Row.
* Dance of Anger, Harriet Goldhor Lerner. Harper & Row, 1985.
* Getting to Yes: Negotiating Agreement Without Giving In, Fisher & Ury. Penguin.
Love is Letting Go of Fear, Gerald G. Jampolsky. Celestial Arts, 1979.
* How to Survive the Loss of a Love, Colgrove, Bloomfield & McWilliams. Bantam.
The Divorce Book, McKay, Rogers, Blades, & Gosse. New Harbinger, 1984.
Uncoupling: the Art of Coming Apart, Mannes & Sheresky. Viking, 1982.

For Parents:
Helping Your Child Succeed After Divorce, Florence Bienenfeld. Hunter House, 1987.
Helping Your Children With Divorce, Edward Teyber, Ph.D.
* Parent's Book About Divorce, Richard A. Gardner. Doubleday, 1977.

* Surviving the Breakup, Wallerstein and Kelly. Basic Books, 1980.
What Every Child Would Like Parents to Know About Divorce, Lee Salk. Warner Books, 1978.

Shared Custody:
* Mom's House, Dad's House, Isolina Ricci. McMillan, 1980.
Sharing Parenthood After Divorce, Ciji Ware. Viking, 1982.

For Fathers:
101 Ways to Be a Long Distance Super-Dad, George Newman. Blossom Valley Press, 1981.
The Father's Role, Ed. by Michael E. Lamb. Wylie & Sons, 1986.

For Scholars:
* The Process of Divorce, Kenneth Kressel. Basic Books, 1985.